CHOICES 2.0

SITUATIONS FOR COLLEGE WRITING

Joe Marshall Hardin

FOUNTAINHEAD
PRESS

D1318973

Our green initiatives include:

Electronic Products
We deliver products in non-paper form whenever possible. This includes PDF down-loadables, flash drives, and CDs.

Electronic Samples
We use Xample, a new electronic sampling system. Instructor samples are sent via a personalized web page that links to PDF downloads.

FSC
FSC Certified Printers
All of our printers are certified by the Forest Service Council which promotes environ-mentally and socially responsible management of the world's forests. This program allows consumer groups, individual consumers and businesses to work together to pro-mote responsible use of the world's forests as a renewable and sustainable resource.

Recycled Paper
Most of our products are printed on a minimum of 30% post consumer waste recycled paper.

Support of Green Causes
When we do print, we donate a portion of our revenue to Green causes. Listed be-low are a few of the organizations that have received donations from Fountainhead Press. We welcome your feedback and suggestions for contributions, as we are always searching for worthy initiatives.
Rainforest 2 Reef
Environmental Working Group

Designer: Susan Moore

Books may be purchased for educational purposes.

For information, please call or write:

1-800-586-0330

Fountainhead Press
Southlake, TX 76092

Web Site: www.fountainheadpress.com
E-mail: customerservice@fountainheadpress.com

Second Edition

ISBN: 978-1-59871-339-8

Printed in the United States of America

TABLE OF CONTENTS

BEFORE YOU BEGIN

As scientists and researchers continue to come up with new information and communication technologies, it becomes increasingly important that citizens and professionals of all kinds be able to communicate well in a wide variety of challenging situations. In this new century, college graduates who know the basics of effective writing and successful argument and who can make use of these new technologies will be much in demand in their professions and in their communities. As such, we have designed *Choices: Situations for College Writing* to bring writing instruction up-to-date with the latest technology and to equip students with proven techniques for creating sentences, paragraphs, visuals, and documents that contain effective narrative, analytical, and argumentative structures.

Many of these effective writing techniques will seem familiar to you. That is because the basics of good writing and argument have not changed that much—even though the way we write and publish documents has changed. Students of only 50 years ago would be amazed by our ability to manipulate text and images on computers, smartphones, and other devices, and they would probably be mystified by the quantity and quality of the information at our fingertips; nevertheless, they would still recognize effective writing and communication techniques. This course is focused on making centuries-old knowledge about how to create effective arguments apply to today's information and communication technologies. In the end, our hope is that you will begin to think in a different way about your writing—a way that includes more consideration of your intended reader and the "situation" in which you are writing. We also hope that the course will help you prepare for the types of writing you may actually encounter in your academic, professional, and civic life.

In return, this course will require that you think beyond the usual way you might have written papers for your previous writing classes. First, the projects you will complete ask that you consider who the readers for the project might be, what those readers might expect from this type of writing, what they might value, and how you can tailor your writing to appeal to those values. Secondly, these projects will ask that you consider how technology can be used to make your writing projects something that you will be proud to have other people read. After all, there is little reason to write something unless someone else is going to read it.

This book is accompanied by an e-portfolio program that allows you to collect both the work you do to prepare for these projects and the final projects. This e-portfolio will help you turn your writing projects into something more than just assignments you did for a class. With the e-portfolio, you can manage and update a "cache" of your writing projects so that you might showcase your abilities as a writer during your academic career, when you are on the job market, or in other situations when you need to demonstrate your abilities. Your e-portfolio will be stored where only you and those you choose will be able to see it, and it will not "time out" or become unavailable. We hope that the e-portfolio will encourage you to produce writing projects that you can be proud of. In the end, it is your education, and you can choose how much you want to get out of it. Choose wisely.

TALENT, HARD WORK, AND CORRECTNESS

> *"I ... believe that words can help us move or keep us paralyzed, and that our choices of language and verbal tone have something—a great deal—to do with how we live our lives and whom we end up speaking with and hearing; and that we can deflect words . . . or we can let them enter our souls and mix with the juices of our minds."--Adrienne Rich*

MAKING CHOICES

Students often come to their college writing classes believing that successful writers just naturally know what and how to write. While a few students may be confident of their abilities, most are actually apprehensive about having to write for a grade. Inexperienced writers often assume that some people are good at expressing themselves in writing, but that most of us struggle to get the ideas in our heads down on paper. When we think of writers we admire, we probably attribute their success to a kind of creativity and expressiveness that most of us do not possess; or we may suspect that their ideas flow magically from some secret place of inspiration.

The early Greeks believed that the daughters of Zeus, called the Muses, provided inspiration for writers, musicians, dancers, and scientists, but modern people believe that some are just more talented at one thing than they are another. In the end, though, using the word "talent" to explain why some people can do things that others cannot is not much better than attributing their success to the Muses. We also tend to think that people are primarily gifted in just one area—that some have talent for music, art, and writing, that others are naturally better at athletics and sports, and that some are destined to excel in math or science. While it may be that some people have physical attributes, patterns of thought, and perhaps even genetic potential to succeed in artistic, athletic, or scientific endeavors, a specific gene for talent or success in any area has not been found—nor is it likely to be. What is more likely is that what is often seen as talent in one area is not a genetic trait at all but a combination of interest, motivation, knowledge, and hard work. In fact, hard work, motivation, and knowledge often enable people who feel they have no natural ability at something to excel at it, while others seem to waste natural ability by not developing it. For an interesting discussion of the relationship between dedication and success, check out Malcolm Gladwell's book, *Outliers* (http://www.gladwell.com/outliers/index.html).

The same relationship between hard work, dedication, and success holds true for writing. Some writers (and even some writing teachers) promote the idea that certain people have a talent for writing and that others simply do not. Perhaps you have been told that you have a talent for writing, or you may believe that you lack the aptitude to be a good writer. Whether you believe you have a talent for writing or not, the evidence is that you can learn to write well enough, regardless of your talent. We are not all destined to become great writers, but we can, if we choose to, learn to write well enough to manage the writing tasks we will encounter in our academic work and in our careers. However, chances are you will never become even a competent writer unless you understand a little bit about how writers work, unless you practice writing, and unless you choose to learn how to do the work of writing.

One thing that we do know about writing is that very rarely does anyone produce an effective piece of writing without hard work. But what are writers actually doing when they work on a piece of writing? In a way, the primary work of a writer is to make choices about what to include and what to exclude, what words to use, and how to organize ideas. While different writers may pose the questions in different ways, most writers begin by asking themselves some form of the following questions:

- ❏ Specifically who or what kind of people will be likely to read this and what are they likely to care about?

- ❏ What can I assume my reader or readers will know before they read and what do I need to explain?

- ❏ Why should my readers care what I have to say about this subject?

- ❏ What kind of logic might convince my readers to believe me or to consider my ideas?

- ❏ What do I want my readers to feel, think, or do after they read this?

Writers may phrase these questions differently, of course. In fact, unless you are used to doing this sort of planning before you write, there may not be any questions occurring in your conscious mind at all as you write. But you are still making choices. If you write without making these choices consciously—just writing off the top of your head—then you are still writing and still making choices, but you are not actively engaging in the *work* of writing. If it remains an off-the-top-of-the-head writing, then you are ignoring the most obvious advantage that writing has over speaking: the opportunity to make choices about what you are going to say before you say it.

Another advantage that writing has over speaking is that it gives you the opportunity to examine what you have written after you have written it in order to make it more effective. This holds true even when you are writing an email or dashing off a quick post to a friend's Facebook page. If you do not think about what you are going to write before you write, then you risk having your words misinterpreted. If you are writing a longer piece then you will likely have to work extra hard to make some sense of the writing after you have written it the first time. The sensible way to approach writing is to do both: first, plan what you are going to write before you write it and then read what you have written afterwards to see if you can make it more effective. **Planning** and **revising**—that is the real work of writing, and that is the work that most beginning writers miss. Virtually everything that you have ever read of any length has been planned and worked on and changed from its original form. Even the most accomplished and "talented" writers make some plan before they begin and then re-work their writing after they complete a first draft, making changes to the structure and tone, throwing sections away, beginning again, and changing and modifying sentences and whole sections. Even short items such as emails and blog posts should be read over and changed until they convey exactly what the writer wants them to convey.

Another trick that successful writers know is that they have to have others read and respond to their work before it is read by "real" readers. As such, most writers have trusted friends and editors that read their drafts to give them feedback on what is working and what is not. Not that writers will automatically make the changes that these readers suggest: good writers maintain control of the final product. However, this practice of having trusted readers is common even in the business and professional worlds, where people's jobs rely on the ability to write clearly. No savvy businessperson or professional will send out a report, a letter, a memo, or perhaps even an email without having someone else read it first. This is simply good writing practice. No matter how many times you read a piece of writing that you have written, you will never be able to see the mistakes and weak passages that another person can see. You have probably noticed that you can read a sentence that you have written several times and still not see that you have left out a word. Another reader might notice instantly that the word has been left out. This practice of having your work read by someone else does not require that the other person be a professional editor, either. All that is necessary is for the reader to agree to read carefully. Additionally, you should learn to read other writers' work as well, for there is much you can learn from seeing the choices that other writers have made. It is easy to trust your eyes when you read, but experienced writers know that it is easy to miss the most obvious omissions and errors.

For example, read the following sentence only once and see how many letter f's you see:

> *Finished files are the result of years of scientific study combined with the experience of years.*

Most people will count only three or four f's on the first reading, but there are actually six. If you caught all six on the first try, you realized that the "of's" in the sentence contained f's as well. Why do you think that this happens?

If you believe in your ability to improve your writing regardless of whether you think you have a natural talent or not, you can learn to write more skillfully and more effectively. Who knows, you may even find that you do have talent for writing. All you had to do was make a choice.

? *Questions for Discussion*

What activity are you good at? Are you good at math, baseball, or making friends? Do you have a good fashion sense, or the ability to play a musical instrument? How much of that ability is based on your interest, your hard work, and your knowledge? How have others influenced your ability to excel in this area? How much does "talent" have to do with your ability?

WHAT ABOUT GRAMMAR?

In addition to the fear that many inexperienced writers have about not being talented, many are also afraid that the words and sentences they write will not be "correct." There is nothing worse than working on a piece of writing and then getting it back from the teacher covered with mysterious red marks highlighting all of your "grammar" mistakes. "Grammar" may seem like a mysterious system of "rules" that only a few can understand, but like the issue of talent, a lack of understanding of what is "correct" and what is "incorrect" can be overcome by a bit of hard work.

If you look at the back of most books about writing, you will find sections of rules. Often, these sections are split up into categories of punctuation, sentence style, and grammar. In these sections, there is usually a rule or a definition given for something like comma splices, use of conjunctions, or subject-verb agreement. These rules are usually stated as things you must or must not do: "Make subjects and verbs agree, even when separated by other words." These rules are generally followed by examples that show sentences that violate this rule and then show how those sentences might be "corrected." Often, the examples are followed by sentences that are done correctly and ones that are done incorrectly and you are asked to correct the incorrect ones. Theoretically, you will then look at your own sentences in the same way to find the "incorrect" ones. Completing these exercises is designed to help you learn to examine your sentences so that you can fix the incorrect "grammar" in your own writing.

The trouble is that this approach often does not work too well. Highly motivated students may be able to transfer to their own writing the knowledge gathered from reading these rules and practicing the corrections, but many students report that this method of learning "grammar" is confusing. While experienced writers will keep one of these grammar books close by to look up suggestions for difficult sentences, most writers do not learn to write by first memorizing all the grammar rules. Once again, this process of learning grammar before writing seems to be aimed at writers who do not possess the "talent" to write naturally. We believe that it is better to think about grammar and "correctness" the way that "real" writers do.

For instance, if you are a person who uses texting or other instant messaging services on your cell phone or smart phone or if you have used or read micro-blogs like Twitter, then you know that an entire system of alternate spelling has been created for texting in order to make the messages shorter. How did you learn what words can be shortened and what words to spell out—that "lol" meant "laughing out loud" or that "brb" means "be right back?" Chances are that you learned these "conventions" of texting by reading what other people had written and trying them out on your own. The truth is that if you have been speaking and listening to English for your entire life then most of the knowledge about how sentences are put together "correctly" is already in your head. You just have to slow down and pay attention to your sentences in order to make use of what you already know.

What "real" writers do is pay attention and make conscious choices about their sentences based on the appropriateness of the language to the situation for which they are writing and then relying first on their sense of what "sounds right." That is right. Although many teachers caution against relying on what sounds right to correct grammar, it is actually a good place to begin as long as you realize that you need lots of writing and reading experience to be really good at knowing what is good by what sounds right. Additionally, you must learn to read your sentences slowly and out loud. Relying on this method—reading your sentences out loud to establish which ones work and which ones do not—will not allow you to catch every error, but at least it's a good place to start. We suggest that you begin by always reading everything you write out loud one sentence at a time. If you read your sentences out loud, slowly, then you can hear much more clearly what the sentences sound like than if you read them silently off the computer screen. If you read a sentence out loud and it does not make sense to you—if it does not say exactly what you wanted it to say—then you need to keep working on it until it does make sense, sound right, and say what you meant. Even if all you are doing is writing one sentence, you should still read it carefully before you send it off to the reader. You have to do more than this to become a competent writer, of course, but this is a good place to start.

In the end, you have to pay more attention to what works for you and what does not. As you write more, you will begin to notice what kinds of mistakes you make. You can then go to the "rule book" to find out how to "correct" that kind of problem. Your teacher and your fellow students can help you identify the types of problems you have and then you can work to fix those problems in particular. Make no mistake about it, though, good writers are concerned with each and every sentence, even if all they are writing is that one sentence. If the sentences do not work then it does not matter how brilliant the ideas are. Readers expect certain kinds of language in certain kinds of writing, too. Readers of academic writing will expect essays where words have been fully written out and not abbreviated as in texting. Likewise, people reading short Tweets or text messages will not expect academic essays to come streaming into their smartphones. Readers in all situations will always expect that sentences will make sense, that they will be appropriate for the situation, and that errors will not get in the way of their understanding what the writer is trying to say. However, there is so much more to writing than memorizing grammar rules. The place to start is with an understanding that good sentences and the use of appropriate conventions are always important, that many problems can be prevented or fixed just by paying attention and by reading out loud, and that effective writers always care about and work on these details.

? *Questions For Discussion*

What rules can you remember teachers giving you about writing and grammar? Make a list of some of these rules and see if you can establish why they have been given to you. For example, how many of your classmates have been told never to use first person (I, me, my, and mine) in a paper? Is this a good rule? Why do you think that some teachers "outlaw" the use of first person?

BEGINNINGS

The important thing to keep in mind as you begin is that the real work of writing is about making choices. Too often, people with little writing experience think that writing is just the thoughts in the writer's head put down on paper, but writing is more than just "talking on the page." Writing gives you the opportunity to choose how to best represent your ideas to the reader. You will need to make choices about what form your writing will take: do you need an instant message, an email, a letter, a report, a story, a short analysis, or a full-blown argumentative essay? With the availability of fully useable images and video on the Internet (check out http://en.wikipedia.org/wiki/Wikimedia_Commons) and access to digital cameras (your cell phone probably has one), you will want to consider whether you need to include an image or even a video to help you communicate. In fact, you might consider whether your topic really needs to be a documentary or a short film uploaded to YouTube. Whatever form your writing takes, you will still need to make choices about how you will present yourself, how you want your readers to think of themselves as they read your text, and about what kind of language and images you will use. These are the real benefits of writing: the ability to think about what you want to write before you write it, the opportunity to make the best representation of yourself in your writing, and the possibility that you may just find a way to make your readers believe or at least be challenged by what you have written.

Whatever talents or faults you may think you have as a writer, you can learn to write more effectively if you take each writing project as a call to make conscious choices.

CHAPTER ONE

MAKING CHOICES ABOUT PROCESS AND RHETORIC

"Excellence, then, is a state concerned with choice . . ."

--Aristotle

MAKING CHOICES ABOUT PROCESS

Somewhere along the path of your academic career you have probably heard reference to something called **the writing process**, which is generally presented as a set of steps that a writer takes in order to create a writing project. Most often, these steps are represented as the stages of **prewriting**, **drafting**, **revising**, and **proofing** (sometimes referred to as **editing**). One of the reasons this model has become popular is because it results from applying the scientific method to research about writing. In the scientific method, scientists first observe something in nature—let us say the growth of plants—and create a model to explain how it works. First, the scientist might observe some plants to analyze what elements must be present for growth. From that observation, the scientist would create a hypothesis that he or she could test: most plants need sunlight, oxygen, nutrients, and water to grow. This list of things that most plants need to grow may seem obvious from observation, but the scientist is not satisfied with a hypothesis based on observation alone. A good hypothesis needs to be tested. In order to test the hypothesis, the scientist might try to grow some plants without one of the elements to see if all four are, in fact, needed. We can easily imagine the results of that experiment: the plants would most likely die. After the experiment, the scientist could then create a model: most plants need all four elements—sunlight, oxygen, nutrients, and water—to grow. With some refinement of that model, the scientist might be confident enough to then call that model a theory. For more information on the scientific method, see http://biology. clc.uc.edu/courses/bio104/SCI_meth.htm.

Researchers have also applied the scientific method to writing. By observing the work of successful writers, researchers developed a model of writing that resulted in a theory about the process of writing. This theory proposes that successful writers do four things: plan before they write, create a first draft, read and rewrite what they have written again to make it better, and then look carefully to make sure all the details have been done correctly. Writing teachers call the steps of this model prewriting, drafting, revising, and proofing. In short, writing researchers took the same steps that scientists take: they observed effective writers, formed a hypothesis about what elements were essential, and created a model and a theory of that process:

❏ Prewriting—in this stage, writers perform some task or tasks that help them plan what they will write.

❏ Drafting—in this stage, writers put something on the page.

❏ Revising—in this stage, writers re-read what they have written and, based on choices about their purpose and intended readers, make major and minor changes to the structure and the sentences.

❏ Proofing—in this stage, writers read what they have written carefully to check for punctuation, spelling, word choice, omitted words, and other "errors." They also check the basic elements of the document's design, such as line spacing, font size, placement of graphics and other visual elements, to see that they are appropriate.

The process approach to teaching writing has been advantageous to writing teachers because it gives them a way to address the processes of individual writers. A plant that is not thriving can often be helped if the gardener can establish what essential elements for growth are out of balance, and a writer who is struggling with a writing project can often be helped if the teacher can establish what elements of the writing process are out of balance.

As they applied the process model, teachers noticed that the processes of inexperienced writers were out of balance in that they generally concentrated on the second and fourth steps—drafting and proofing—and did not pay enough attention to the first and third steps—prewriting and revising. What is interesting about this is that it is in the steps of prewriting and revising where the most choices about what and how to write are made. That is why we believe that students can improve their writing if they concentrate on making choices before they write and after they have written.

As teachers were applying the process model, they also noticed that there were a wide variety of ways that successful writers employed the steps of this process. Just as various types of plants have adapted differently to their environments, writers have come up with variations on the writing process that are highly individualized. Some people also revise and proof as they draft, and some people go back to the prewriting stage after drafting to come up with new material. Researchers and teachers also noticed that most writers do not complete each step of the process before they move on to the next step and then never return to the previous step. So writing researchers decided two things about the process model. First, they decided that the steps are **recursive**, which means that they often overlap and fold back upon each other. For example, writers often do some initial revising and proofing while they are drafting. Second, researchers decided that there was no single "writing process." Instead, they noticed that there are many processes that writers use to successfully create effective writing. While all writers seem to do something that corresponds to each stage of the model, these processes are different for each writer—so much so that researchers and teachers began to speak about "writing processes" instead of "the writing process."

Now, most researchers and teachers believe that every writer must develop his or her own processes. Still, experience suggests that the two areas of writing where inexperienced writers need the most help are in thinking about what they will write before they write it and in making significant changes after they have completed an initial draft. If you think about it, it is easy to understand why this is so: planning and revising are the stages of any writing process where the majority of choices are made. True, you can just begin to write and see what comes out, but if you do, then you are still making unconscious or split-second choices as you draft, and you will have to make even more conscious and thoughtful choices in the revision stage.

Prewriting

There are some logical ways to proceed with any writing project, and over the years, various writers and writing teachers have suggested some special techniques to use, especially in the early stages of the project—in the prewriting stage. These established techniques include various strategies of **list-making**, **idea-clustering**, **outlining**, **freewriting**, and **journaling**. You have probably heard about some of these techniques or perhaps learned to use them yourself:

> **List-making**: One way to plan for a writing project is to simply make a list of your major ideas and then list below or next to those major ideas what your supporting ideas and points might be. Often, list-making will help you decide whether you have enough or too much information for your project and where you need to add more of your own ideas or more support for them.

Idea-clustering: Idea-clustering is similar to list-making except the major idea for the writing project is generally put in the center of the paper and the supporting ideas are arranged around the major idea with spokes to connect them. Further supports for those ideas are then arranged around them. The effect is much like creating a map of your writing project with each idea occupying a specific space on the page.

Outlining: A good, legible outline can be a terrific map for a writing project. Most of us have created outlines for writing projects before. While some teachers and writers obsess over outline form, with proper numbering schemes for the outline, and with the way the elements of the outline line up on the page, we suggest thinking of an outline as a kind of list in which items are indented to show how they are grouped under or equivalent to other ideas. You can use a standard numbering and lettering system for an outline, but we suggest not getting too tangled up in "proper" outline form unless your teacher requires it. Still, remember that you are trying to create a writing project and not a perfect outline.

Freewriting: Freewriting is sitting in front of the computer or with pen and paper and just writing without stopping. This form of prewriting works for some people, but there are two dangers that come with this technique. The first is that the writer will just get bogged down with nothing to say. To overcome this, you have to be willing to keep on writing, even if you have to write "I can't think of anything to write at this point," or something like that. The other danger is that some inexperienced writers will believe that whatever has been done during freewriting is good enough to constitute a sufficient draft. Freewriting almost always needs extensive revision just to make a decent first draft. If you freewrite, then you probably need to be willing to do much more revision than if you had done any other form of prewriting.

Journaling: Many writers use some kind of journaling to keep themselves "warmed up" for their writing projects. Journaling can be an especially effective way to prewrite because it gives the writer a way to test out ideas, sentences, and strategies before committing to a large project. Although many writers keep private journals, an increasing number use **blogging** to test out their writing on real readers in a more informal context. In this course, for example, you will be encouraged to create your own blog where you can "warm up" for your writing projects and test out your ideas. So many people blog now (including most writing professionals) that blogging and video blogging have themselves become genres of writing. In addition to the blog site that accompanies this course, there are sites such as Blogger (http://www.blogger.com) and Wordpress (http://www.wordpress.org) where you can set up your own blogs. Some people have set up video blogs at sites such as Youtube (http://www.youtube.com). Social networking sites such as Facebook (http://www.facebook.com) and MySpace (http://www.myspace.com) are really forms of organized blogging, and Twitter (http://www.twitter.com) is a form of micro-blogging. There are sites such as Flickr (http://www.flickr.com) and Fotolog (http://www.fotolog.com) where you can keep a photoblog. In this case, the blog you will construct for this class will take your writing projects as the subject for the blog. If you subscribe to one of the social networking sites, post original videos to Youtube, keep your photos at an on-line site, or Twitter, though, you are already a blogger.

You may notice that each of these forms of prewriting is a way to find out what the major ideas of the project will be and how they will be supported. Prewriting is also a way to establish how your ideas might be grouped together, what order they need to come in, and whether you have enough or too few ideas. All of these forms of prewriting are simply ways to begin a writing project, and experienced writers find out for themselves which ones work for them and which ones work best for various kinds of writing projects.

For example, some experienced writers will use an outline specifically for writing projects that require sources because the visual structure of an outline helps them decide how to balance and distribute the sources throughout the paper and to determine which parts of the project need more outside support. In fact, some writers will go back and create an outline of something they have already written to see if each portion of the project has been developed sufficiently. Outlining can be a very effective way to establish what parts of a writing project need more work. For other types of projects, writers might make lists or do idea-clustering. Often, writers will employ several different types of prewriting for a single project. Prewriting techniques can also be employed while you draft to help you find new ideas in the middle of the project.

Each of these prewriting techniques helps the writer imagine the project in its finished state. Idea-clustering and outlining are particularly useful for visualizing what the major sections of a project will be and for getting a sense of the length of the project. In fact, if you are worried about your projects not being long enough (or being too long!) you will want to spend more time prewriting so that you can determine just how much material you have before you begin. Blogging is extremely useful for writers of all levels of experience because it helps to keep the "creative juices" flowing and gives the writer a safe zone in which to try out ideas and sentences. Whatever prewriting technique you choose to employ, remember that prewriting is only the first step in the project. Do not get bogged down. If one technique does not work, try another.

Drafting

At some point, you will need to leave the prewriting stage and begin to put the ideas into sentences and the sentences into paragraphs. Inexperienced writers may be tempted to employ freewriting as a prewriting activity because it seems like an easy shortcut through the prewriting stage and directly to the drafting stage. Freewriting is not the same thing as drafting, though. In fact, many people who experience what is often called "writer's block" do so because they skip the prewriting stage and attempt to create a draft of a project without a real plan. Inexperienced writers sometimes report a sense of dread when they sit in front of a blank computer screen or a blank sheet of paper. This is why we suggest that you try at least some form of prewriting before you begin to draft and not to think of freewriting in the same way you think of drafting. Since most inexperienced writers tend to skip the planning stage, we suggest that you blog and journal as much as possible for the projects. Whatever you choose to do, remember that drafting requires some sort of plan. Drafting without prewriting is like trying to build a house without a blueprint.

Developing a plan for your draft and journaling or blogging is also a sure-fire way to avoid serious writer's block. Once you have some prewriting—created a plan for your project—then you can rely on that plan to keep you moving through the drafting stage. As you draft you can look back at your prewriting or at your blog for an idea of what needs to come next and you can check to see that you have not left anything out. Truly, the more you visualize your project before you begin and the more you blog, the more likely you will be able to keep going as you draft. Most inexperienced writers are afraid that they will not have enough words to complete the assignment, and this fear can inhibit the drafting part of the process or it can cause the writer to simply begin to repeat themselves or to add extraneous and "off-topic" ideas. Prewriting and blogging before drafting is a way to prevent that from happening. If you are fearful about getting bogged down with writer's block while you are drafting or if you are fearful about having enough words to complete the writing project, then it is imperative that you engage in some prewriting activity and blogging before you begin to draft.

Another thing to remember is that a draft is just a draft. You can stop in the middle of drafting and return to your prewriting activities, you can leave the whole project for a while and then come back to it (especially if you have a written plan), or you can simply return to freewriting and write anything you can think of just to keep going. After all, it is just a draft and not the final project.

Revising

The term "revision" indicates that it is necessary for the writer to literally re-vision the writing—to see the writing with "fresh eyes." Many writers mistake proofing and editing for revision, but in order to revise a writing project, it is necessary for the writer to be willing to make substantial changes to the project based on reading the writing project as if he or she had never seen it before. You might be shocked by how many inexperienced writers will turn in a writing project without reading it at all. Why would any writer expect that a reader would be interested in reading a writing project that the writer had not even bothered to read?

In order to revise sufficiently, we would suggest that you consider following this procedure:

1. Print a copy of the project so that you can read it from the paper. Reading specialists have discovered that reading on a computer screen and reading from a piece of paper (a hard copy, as it is called) are very, very different. All readers notice different types of things in hard copy than they will notice on screen. You can revise on the computer, but you should also revise after having read from a printed copy.

2. Wait a while after drafting before you begin the revision process. If you are really to "re-vision" the project, it will help if you take some time—a few minutes, an hour, a day—away from the project. This only makes it easier for you to read it as if you are seeing it for the first time.

3. Commit to making substantial changes. To revise a project substantially you must be willing to change the order of things, the basic structure, perhaps even the main idea of the project. Experienced writers know that writing about a topic will often allow them to figure out exactly what it is they think about the subject and that they might even change their point of view significantly about an issue by writing about it.

4. Have the writing project peer-reviewed. As we have said, experienced writers know that having someone else read their work can be extremely beneficial to their writing processes. We have designed these projects so that peer-review is an integral part of each. This is not an academic exercise; this is what "real" writers do. Keep in mind that the feedback you get from colleagues who have

read your work in the draft stage is some of the most important information you can get. These are real readers reacting to your words. Listen to what they say about your writing. Ask them questions. Use their responses and suggestions to help you decide what parts of your writing projects need to be revised and what kind of changes you need to make.

Proofing and Editing

Making sure that your writing is ready for real readers means more than just running the spellchecker over your work, although that is an excellent place to begin. Incidentally, now that almost all writers have access to word-processors with spellchecking, most readers will consider obviously misspelled words to be insulting. Make sure you run the spellchecker (see the supplement for problems with spellcheckers). After you have run the spellchecker, though, there is still proofing work to be done, and we recommend that you once again print out a hard-copy of your project and read it out loud. As we have said, listening to the sentences and the paragraphs as you read them will help you to hear the jumbled sentences and the confusing passages, and it will help you recognize where you have left out words or made other keystroke errors. There is lots of good advice about how to "correct" your sentences or improve your style—we have included several sections on these things in the supplements accompanying this text. Still, you will be surprised by how much improvement you can make if you simply read your work out loud, and how much improvement you can make if you are simply willing to make changes to your sentences until they sound right to you.

Once again, you should notice that it is the choices that the writer makes throughout these processes that matter. What is important is that as you learn to become a more effective writer you develop a conscious awareness of what processes work best for you. What is also important is that you learn to concentrate on the parts of your own individualized writing process where you make choices about what you will write and how you will write it. As you might imagine, taking control of your writing processes takes work and it takes time. You must be willing to start planning your projects when they are assigned and not waiting until the last minute. You must be willing to do more than just throw some words on the page, run the spellchecker, and then turn it in. If you are willing to do the work, though, the payoff will be great. Before you can begin this work, however, it will also help if you know what kind of choices are available to you as a writer and why certain choices are better for one situation than for another.

How much do you know about your own writing processes and writing habits? Do you need it to be absolutely quiet in order to write or do you need a bit of noise? Do you write better in the morning or in the evening? What kind of prewriting activities do you usually do? How do you think about revision? How do your processes compare to other students' processes?

MAKING CHOICES ABOUT RHETORIC

Aristotle, the Greek philosopher, proposed a system for creating arguments that is amazingly similar to the process model of writing. Aristotle was primarily concerned with making speeches, however, and not with writing. In Aristotle's time, very few people had the tools and the ability to write things down, but the need to make speeches was of paramount importance, as in the early Greek form of democracy each individual citizen had to argue his own case before the other citizens. In fact, Aristotle discovered so much about how successful arguments were made that we still rely on his theories today (we also still rely on many of his discoveries about science and literature).

At this point, we need to introduce the term **rhetoric**. Most people have heard this term in one of two ways: either in the phrase "rhetorical question" or in discussions about politics. First, let us examine the idea of the rhetorical question. Generally, a rhetorical question is one that either does not require an answer, or it is a question in which the answer is somehow suggested by the question. For example, let us imagine that you have arrived late for your job and your boss asks "do you think that you can get here anytime you want to?" Of course, your boss does not really believe that you think you can come to work at any time you like. So why would he or she ask that question? The answer is, of course, that your boss wants you to admit that you need to arrive on time. In other words, the question was asked to produce a specific answer: "no, of course I'm supposed to be here at a certain time. I'm sorry I was late, and it won't happen again." In other words, the answer to the hypothetical question is suggested by the question itself. For further information on rhetorical questions, visit the entry on Rhetorical Questions at a site called *Silva Rhetoricae* ,which is sponsored by Brigham Young University (http://rhetoric.byu.edu/figures/R/rhetorical%20questions.htm).

Teachers also ask rhetorical questions, and they do so primarily to make students think. For instance, your teacher might ask "why is making choices important to any successful piece of writing?" Your answer, based on your reading so far, might be something like "making choices is important because it is where the real work of writing gets done." The question, then, already suggests that making choices *is* important. The rhetorical question suggests what the answer to the question will be.

The other place where we hear the word "rhetoric" is in political discussions. You may have heard people say "that's just more of the rhetoric of the political right," or "we need something more than just rhetoric from these politicians." In this case, rhetoric has a somewhat negative connotation in that it suggests that certain positions along the political spectrum (left, right, liberal, conservative, etc.) produce the same sorts of arguments over and over. The implication is that rhetoric is just more of the same kind of talk we have already heard.

Actually, though, the idea of rhetoric is much more complex than either of these two examples suggests. The problem is that the word has gathered a mostly negative connotation, possibly because people have a tendency to believe that anyone who is a skillful speaker, one who can employ rhetoric well, is not to be trusted. This is why people are sometimes more influenced by those who appear to be speaking without thinking too much. The truth is that we often like and trust people who speak "plainly" and who appear to be speaking "off-the-cuff," and we sometimes distrust those whose language appears to be too "polished" or too "slick." Almost everyone who is a successful communicator is adept at rhetoric, though. Even the choice to speak plainly and to avoid jargon and complex arguments is a rhetorical choice, whether that choice is made consciously or unconsciously. At any rate, we prefer to avoid the negative connotation and use the term **rhetoric** simply to refer to **the strategic use of language**. Rhetoric, at least in the context of this course, is the art of thinking about what you are going to write before you write it and refining your language after you have written. Rhetoric helps you:

- ❏ Make choices about how you will present yourself in your writing.

- ❏ Make choices about how you will address your reader.

- ❏ Make choices about what kinds of language and arguments you will use to communicate with or to persuade your reader.

From this perspective, rhetoric refers to the act of making conscious choices to make your language as effective as it can be.

Interestingly, the argument about whether the ability to use rhetoric effectively is a good or a bad thing is an ancient one, too. In ancient Greece, philosophers such as Plato and his former student Aristotle both thought that the ability to use language effectively was one of the most important faculties anyone could possess. Both worried whether individuals of questionable character should be taught rhetoric at all. Plato believed that rhetoric was such a powerful too that only people with the right sort of character should be taught to use it, whereas, Aristotle believed that learning rhetoric would improve a person's character.

Questions For Discussion

What do you think about the idea that only "good" people should be taught to use rhetoric effectively? Do you agree that learning to argue effectively might make you a better person? Can you think of "good" people who are not effective speakers and "bad" people who are?

THE RHETORICAL TRIANGLE

Along with developing a process model for speeches, Aristotle also outlined a method by which speakers could relate more effectively to their listeners. Aristotle's model suggests that speakers can use specific kinds of arguments to appeal to the attitudes, beliefs, and values of various kinds of listeners. He believed that the key to constructing a persuasive speech (or a writing project in our case) is in making good choices about the key elements of the speech. Aristotle came up with a visual aid to help the speaker consider his or her rhetoric before speaking, and this visual aid is still in use today.

Aristotle believed that the three points of the triangle—the speaker, the listener, and the speech—influenced each other and that all three points revolved around the subject matter. Although he was primarily concerned with making speeches, we can easily transfer his ideas to the act of writing. According to Aristotle then, writers can make their arguments more effective if they consider, before they write, who the reader might be. Then, they can make choices about how to best relate their knowledge of the subject and their arguments to those readers. Readers generally already know something about the subject, or they have certain expectations of what might be written about the subject. As such, writers must think about how to create a text that takes into account what readers' values and expectations are in order to effectively communicate new ideas about the subject. A good **rhetor**, which is the term used for

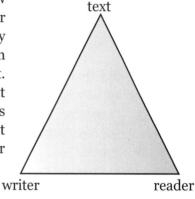

text

writer   reader

someone employing the ideas of rhetoric, would consider the relationship between all three points on the triangle.

Each specific point on Aristotle's rhetorical triangle deserves careful consideration. Writers must consider who their readers might be and what values and expectations they might have. Then, writers can make choices about how to make the best presentation of themselves and their ideas. Additionally, effective rhetors must ask themselves the question, "why will my readers care what *I* have to say about this issue." What can I, as a writer, bring to the issue that will encourage my listener to grant that I am credible?

A ▶ *Activity*

Imagine that you are going to try and persuade your school to add more parking spaces for students. How would your argument differ as you tried to persuade other students and then the administrators of your school? Would you emphasize different points of the argument for the two different groups? Why? Would you make a different presentation of your credibility to each group? How? What values would you emphasize in your argument to the students and would they differ from the values you would emphasize in your argument to the administration? You might form small groups and have each group write a short summary of the argument for more parking spaces as you would present it to students. Then, write another short summary of the argument for more parking spaces as you would present it to the administration.

THE THREE APPEALS

Aristotle believed that rhetors must "relate" their argument to their reader in three ways. In order to see how this works, let us put ourselves in the reader's spot on the triangle and think about what convinces us. If you are like most people, you will assume that statistics, facts, and logic are what counts. Aristotle also believed that statistics, facts, and logic are important for any successful argument, and he advised the skillful rhetor to appeal to the audience using good logic. Aristotle called this the appeal to **logos**. The word *logos*, in fact, looks very much like the English word "logic." Actually, the word *logos* can be most accurately translated from the ancient Greek language as the English word for either "voice" or "speech." However, we probably would recognize what Aristotle was referring to in our ideas of rationality and logic. An argument that has sufficient appeals to *logos* is one that is "logical" and "rational." However, Aristotle suggested that arguments that appealed to the rationality of the reader—that relied on the proper presentation of statistics, logic, and facts—are only partially complete. He also suggested that readers respond to their emotions as they read a piece of writing or listen to a speaker.

The idea that readers respond with their emotions as they read may be somewhat surprising, as we tend to think of rationality and emotion as contradictory terms and to assume that any appeal to the emotions is "cheap" or inappropriate to a good argument. Still, Aristotle understood that readers, even though they might believe that they are primarily rational beings, also *do* respond with their emotions, especially when they are praised or threatened. Aristotle called this the appeal to **pathos**. The word *pathos* most closely translates to the English word "experience," but Aristotle linked the audience's emotions so closely to what they had experienced that he eventually used the word *pathos* to mean any emotional state in the audience. We can see the influence of this idea in our words "sym*pathy*" and "em*pathy*," two words that suggest an emotional connection. So Aristotle suggested that the effective rhetor made appeals to the audiences' logic and rationality and to their emotions.

Aristotle believed that the personal character of the rhetor was also highly influential. In fact, he suggested that unless the audience trusted that the rhetor's intentions and credibility were good, the appeals to logic and emotion would most likely fail, no matter how effective they were. Aristotle called this kind of credibility the appeal to **ethos**, and the influence of this word can be seen in our modern word "ethics." So, the rhetor must be perceived as an ethical person in order for the logic and the emotion of the argument to be accepted by the audience. Of the three appeals, Aristotle believed that the appeal to *ethos* was the most important. Still, he suggested that any effective speech (or writing project) should contain appropriate appeals to *ethos*, *pathos*, and *logos*--credibility, emotion, and logic.

Although various types of argument call for rhetoric that emphasizes one or the other of the three appeals, it is generally best to consider all three when you construct your writing:

❏ The appeal to *ethos*—the writer's credibility.

❏ The appeal to *pathos*—the reader's emotions.

❏ The appeal to *logos*—the logic of the argument or persuasion.

Do you agree with Aristotle that the writer's credibility is the key to whether or not a reader will believe in the logic and emotion of an argument? Can you think of a case in which you have valued a person's opinion even though you did not trust them? How did that differ from a time when you believed in a person's opinion and you did trust that the person was credible?

A SAMPLE ARGUMENT

Let us examine how Aristotle's three appeals might be used effectively. Suppose that we wanted to make an argument about adult literacy to an audience of college students. Since our basic impulse is to begin with the appeal to logic, and we can assume that any college reader would want to have some rational reason to accept our argument, let us begin by basing our argument on a fact:

Because 14 percent of American adults are illiterate, we should work to make sure that all American adults are able to read and write.

Obviously, much is missing in the above "argument," and there is much that we could add to make it better. First, we might build both our appeal to logic and credibility by citing the source for the statistic. The intelligent reader's first question is likely to be "who says that 14 percent of American adults are illiterate?" So let us add some information about where we obtained our statistic:

According to a U.S. Department of Education survey conducted in 2003 and published on the website of the National Center for Education Statistics, 14 percent of American adults are illiterate. As such, we should work to make sure that all American adults are able to read and write.

We have now given the reader a reason to believe our statistic by citing the source. This also reinforces the logical appeal because it seems logical that we would turn to a reputable source like the Department of Education for information on illiteracy. That, of course, also reinforces our credibility, our *ethos*, as our readers are more likely to trust us because we have cited a reputable source. Still, astute readers will want to know as much about a statistic as possible. As you are aware, statistics and facts can be twisted and manipulated to produce many different effects, which is why the appeals to *logos* and *ethos* work best together: if we expect readers to trust a fact or statistic then we need to convince them that it comes from a good source and that we have presented it honestly and fairly. After all, the same statistics and facts can be presented in ways that support either side of an argument. Instead of writing that 14 percent of Americans are illiterate, we could have said that 86 percent of Americans *are* literate.

There is still a bit of a problem with the statistic, though. What does the term "illiterate" mean? Does it mean that 14 percent of Americans cannot read or write at all? It would help with the *logos* and the *ethos* if we defined the term. In fact, if we look at the survey more carefully (http://nces.ed.gov/NAAL/PDF/2006470_1.PDF), we can see that it defines illiteracy as the inability to "search, comprehend, and use" information from a written text. Examples of activities that "illiterate" people cannot accomplish include reading a message from a doctor about how to provide treatment for a sick family member, figuring out where to sign their name to an official form, and adding up the numbers on a bank deposit slip. By supplying this specific definition of literacy as it is used in the survey, we increase our credibility, reinforce our appeal to logic, and add an appeal to emotions (*pathos*). After all, readers might sympathize with people who are illiterate if they can imagine just what it is that they cannot do.

Emotional appeals can also be reinforced by the use of specific words, and we can strengthen the emotional appeal by suggesting a possible emotional response for the reader. Let us add the description of illiteracy to our argument in order to reinforce the logical and the emotional appeal, and let us suggest an emotional response by adding the word "tragically":

According to a U.S. Department of Education survey conducted in 2003 and published on the website of the National Center for Education Statistics, 14 percent of American adults are illiterate. Tragically, this means that these people cannot follow the written directions of their doctors, figure out where to sign their name to an official form, or add up the simple numbers on a bank deposit slip. As such, we should work to make sure that all American adults are able to read and write.

Much better. Still, as Aristotle suggests, we should always work to make our appeal to *ethos*, our credibility, more effective. One of the ways that Aristotle suggests that we establish credibility is by attempting to "relate" to the reader, to make them feel as though "we" are all in this together. So far, we have simply suggested that some unknown "we" should address the problem of adult illiteracy in America. Let us consider our reader a bit more. We have suggested in our argument that this is an "American" problem, and we might be tempted to suggest that the concerned group that we all belong to is the group called "Americans." However, we might encourage the reader to form a stronger bond with us by pointing out more things that we have in common. We suggested that the reader for this argument would be a college audience, so we might point to that relationship by writing "*we, as American college students, should work to make sure that all American adults are able to read and write.* " We might also suggest how we could work together to accomplish this goal. As it is, we have not really made much of a suggestion for a solution. Anyone can complain about a problem, cite statistics, and suggest that "something" should be done, but what if we could suggest a way to actually help? One possible proposal might be that college students should volunteer in a literacy program. So let us put this all together:

According to a U.S. Department of Education survey conducted in 2003 and published on the website of the National Center for Education Statistics, 14 percent of American adults are illiterate. Tragically, this means that these people cannot follow the written directions of their doctors, figure out where to sign their name to an official form, or add up the simple numbers on a bank deposit slip. As such, we, as American college students, should consider volunteering in a local adult literacy program to make sure that all American adults are able to read and write.

Compare this form of the argument—after we have worked on it using Aristotle's appeals to consciously reinforce the argument's *ethos*, *pathos*, and *logos*—to the original:

Because 14 percent of American adults are illiterate, we should work to make sure that all American adults are able to read and write.

It would be easier to work some of these choices out before we began to write our argument, but even working with the argument we had already constructed, we were able to greatly improve its effectiveness by considering what the reader might expect and by strengthening the appeals to *ethos*, *pathos*, and *logos*.

UNDERSTANDING THE KEY CONCEPTS

1. What are the four stages of the writing process, how were they developed, and which two can the inexperienced writer concentrate on to make his or her writing more effective?

2. Why do we now say that there are "writing processes" instead of just one "writing process," and why do we now say that the stages of individual writing processes are "recursive?"

3. What is your understanding of the word "rhetoric" and what is a "rhetor?"

4. What is Aristotle's rhetorical triangle and how can we use it to make more effective writing?

5. What are Aristotle's three appeals and how do they work? Which of the three appeals did Aristotle suggest was the most important and why?

✓ CHECKLIST OF QUESTIONS FOR PROCESS

1. Did you do any significant prewriting for your writing project?

2. What form did that prewriting take?

3. Did you give yourself significant time to draft the essay? How much time?

4. Have you done significant revision making changes, if needed, to the structure and tone?

5. Did you read your sentences aloud, listening for problems and correcting them?

6. Have you had someone else read your writing project and offer suggestions?

- Targeted audience that isn't the teacher

HOMEPAGE PROJECT

Your "homepage" will serve as the initial page that readers will use to access your blog and your completed projects for this class. Your homepages will generally serve as a site to welcome your readers and as a "portal" to the major contents of your website--in this case, as the portal to your blog and to your projects. Your homepage should reflect the content of the website and provide links to the major pages and projects of the site.

Setting Up Your Homepage

In preparation for setting up your homepage, write a short biographical sketch about yourself of no more than 250 to 350 words. In this entry, you might give the reader some important information such as where you are originally from, past academic experience, current academic interests, hobbies (favorite bands, movies, and books or writers, for example), extra-curricular activities, and anything else that might give the reader a sense of "who you are." Your biographical entry should give the reader a sense of your personality, too. You can adjust the tone of the biographical sketch to reflect your general outlook on life—are you a person who generally uses humor; are you a generally serious person? The tone should, of course, reflect your general outlook on life. Keep in mind, however, that your entry should also reflect a consideration of your reader. What will make your reader want to enter your site and view your projects? How will you generate that interest with your short biographical sketch? Be sure to read your sentences out loud, have the members of your peer response group read and comment on your sketch, and revise and proofread it carefully.

The Visual Element

When you login to the Choices web portal to construct your homepage, you will be asked to provide a photograph. You may want to supply a "headshot," which is a photograph that contains primarily a picture of your face. However, you may wish to use a photograph of yourself that alludes to your interests or your general outlook. You may have a photo of yourself at the beach or in the mountains that you wish to use, or you may have a photo of yourself dancing with your friends or at a party or standing in front of your car or with a favorite pet. Choose the photo that you will use carefully, though, to set the tone for your website--keeping in mind that the website will feature your work as a writer and as a college student. Consider carefully how the photo that you select reflects you and this particular set of projects.

This is also a good place to begin a discussion of how visuals can contribute to the credibility, to the emotional content, and to the logic of a document. As you select the photo for your homepage, ask yourself what the picture you are posting contributes to the overall message of the homepage. What will the photograph you choose to upload say about who you are? Will the picture encourage your reader to take your homepage seriously? How will the photo contribute to the overall message that you wish to give your reader about what you value and what you hope to accomplish with your homepage? As we gain the capability of publishing more and more photographs and images on the web, we need to pay more attention to what messages we are sending to the world about ourselves. While it may be tempting to portray yourself as a party animal, a brooding goth, or a gun-toting mercenary now, how will that image continue to affect your ethos four or five years from now when you are applying for a job?

CHAPTER TWO

MAKING CHOICES ABOUT EXIGENCY, GENRE, AND READERSHIP

> *"Rhetoric may be defined as the faculty of observing in any given case the available means of persuasion."*
>
> *--Aristotle*

EXIGENCY, TOPIC, AND GENRE

Writers generally begin by thinking about the situation for their writing. In writing theory, the term for the situation that motivates a writer to write is **exigency**. The most obvious exigency for writing in any writing course is, of course, the assignment and the course itself. After all, the initial reason that you will be writing is because you have been given an assignment. In order to learn how to construct effective writing, however, you should begin to think beyond this limited classroom exigency, to imagine a "real" reader for your writing projects.

When writers begin to think about the exigency for their writing, they are asking crucial questions that will guide them as they begin to write. Whether writers are aware of what they are doing or not, as soon as they begin to think about what they are going to write, they are formulating the situation, or exigency, for their writing.

In order to establish the exigency for your writing projects, you will need to come up with a topic and establish what kind of writing it will be. Choosing a topic that is appropriate is crucial, and each writing project for this course will guide you through a topic selection process, but selecting a topic is only a small part of setting up the exigency for your writing. For now, let us examine some of the other elements that form the exigency for your writing.

First, you will need to decide what kind of text, what **genre**, your writing will be. For those unfamiliar with the word, "genre" describes the different categories of texts that are available to writers. For instance, letters, emails, reports, websites, essays, articles, and books are all genres—or categories—of non-fiction writing. Novels, short stories, poems, and plays are all genres of fiction writing. As new writing technologies become available, new genres come into use as well. Now, blogging, Tweeting, Facebooking, instant messaging, video blogging, and countless other genres of writing are emerging. It only makes sense that writers need to decide from the beginning what form of communication and which of these genres is the appropriate one for the specific message they are sending. It might be simple to decide that a particular idea needs to be communicated in a letter or an email instead of a formal report or a book, but deciding whether to communicate in an email or a letter might be a more difficult choice.

Obviously, various genres are more appropriate for different types of messages. You probably would not, for instance, want to send your boss a link to your Facebook page or a "tweet" to ask for a raise. Nor would you want to break up with your steady date this way (although there are many stories about people who "dumped" their significant others simply by changing their "relationship status" on Facebook). Blogs are appropriate for some types of personal information, but there is a fine line between the type of self-reflection appropriate for a blog and "too much information." As we develop more and more means of communication and more and more genres of writing, attention to what is and what is not appropriate becomes increasingly important.

In addition, writers must consider that what seems appropriate today may become inappropriate in the future. You may find yourself at a later date regretting some pictures or blogs entries. Always consider that once something is posted to the web it may become permanently available. That is why the blog, homepage, and projects you publish for this course will remain available only to those you choose. Still, we recommend you take this opportunity to think about just how you want to portray yourself to the public.

Even within specific genres, writers still have choices to make. Readers will expect each genre of writing to adhere to certain **conventions** (the word "convention" refers to the way things are normally done), and readers will at least partially evaluate the writing by how those conventions are effectively used or ignored. Readers of academic essays, for instance, may expect a certain level of formality in the language, a certain type of clarity and coherence, certain aspects of design (double spacing, headers, page numbers, no IM language, etc.), and certain structures of support and evidence for the ideas. However, even within the genre of the standard academic essay, there are choices to make about the way you present your ideas, about the way you use the appeals of *ethos*, *logos*, and *pathos*, about the type of language you use, about the design elements, about the values you address, and about the structures you employ. The first questions that need to be asked in order to establish the exigency for your writing might be formulated as follows:

❏ What is the purpose of the writing? What do I hope to accomplish?

❏ What genre should the writing be? A letter? An email? A blog entry? An essay?

Often, the purpose of the writing is referred to as the **thesis**. You should not confuse the topic of your paper with the idea of the thesis. If you think back to the sample paragraph from the last chapter, you will remember that the topic was adult literacy. Our thesis was a specific argument we were making about adult literacy and a particular action that we wanted our reader to take. There was a purpose and something we wanted to accomplish. Instead of thinking first about a thesis statement for your writing projects, it may be more useful if you think about the purpose of your writing, which will then lead you to your thesis statement. The question to ask is this: what do you want the reader to think, feel, or do when he or she finishes reading your writing? If you always keep in mind that you will have an actual reader for your project, you can put your thesis, your purpose for writing, in terms of how you hope to influence your reader's thoughts or feelings with your project or what you want your reader to do or consider doing. You do not necessarily have to plan to change your reader's mind completely, either, or get them to do something they might not ordinarily do. You might simply want to make them think a bit more about the topic, especially to think about the topic in a certain way, or merely to consider your recommendations for action. In the sample argument from the last chapter, we actually wound up by writing what could easily be called a thesis statement or purpose for the writing project:

> *As such, we, as American college students, should consider volunteering in a local adult literacy program to make sure that all American adults are able to read and write.*

As you can see, this thesis addresses the reader directly and challenges them to take some specific action. This thesis clearly states our purpose for writing.

This sort of thesis may be completely different from the way you have thought about the thesis statements before. You may have heard that thesis statements must always come at the end of the first paragraph, that they must always contain the major points of the essay (usually three), that they must be contained in one sentence, and that the writer always needs to establish a perfect and unchangeable thesis statement before beginning the project. Surveys of writers and of actual essays of all sorts suggest that writers approach the idea of the thesis statement in various ways. We suggest that if you can write down exactly what you want the essay to accomplish in one or two sentences then you have a good start on a thesis statement for your writing project. The thesis or purpose of your writing project does not always have to be contained in one sentence, although it should be clear and concise. We also suggest that you go ahead and tell the reader early on—on the first page or so—what the purpose of your writing project is. Still, there is no rule that says that you must put the thesis statement at the end of the first paragraph. Most importantly, you should put yourself in the reader's place: would you read very long if you could not establish what a writer was trying to say to you about a particular topic?

Another thing to consider is that the purpose of your writing project might actually change from the time you begin to plan it and when you finish it. As you are revising, you should look very, very closely to find exactly where you have stated your purpose or placed your thesis statement to establish if that is actually what you have done in the writing project. Do not be afraid to change this part of your project to reflect what you have actually wound up doing as opposed to what you originally planned to do.

? *Questions For Discussion:*

What do you already know about the genre of academic writing? Can you list some of the conventions that readers generally expect of academic writing? What do you know about creating a thesis for your essays and how does that idea differ from creating a purpose for your essay?

THE IDEAL COMMUNITY OF READERS

Too often, inexperienced writers, especially those who are working in an academic setting, do not ask enough questions to establish an exigency for their writing before they begin. They simply write their essays in response to the class assignment, and they choose their tone, language, and structure based on what they think the teacher expects. Although the most obvious goal of the writing done in a writing class is to respond to an assignment, making choices about your writing project simply to satisfy the teacher will not often produce a truly effective piece of writing; nor will it give you the kinds of writing experiences that will help you after you leave the classroom. In fact, it is likely that your teacher will be more impressed with your writing if you have worked out the exigency for your project and if you have chosen the tone, language, and structures in order to work within a clearly defined situation for your writing and not just to complete the assignment. The projects that we have designed to go along with this book are arranged to help you write just these kinds of projects.

As you begin to think about who might read your writing project, you will, of course, want to remember that the teacher will be the one who is evaluating and grading your work. However, you may also want to consider that your classmates will read your work as part of the peer response requirement. You might first begin to expand your thinking beyond simply writing for the teacher by considering how your classmates might respond to your projects once you have published them to your website. There are also readers beyond your teacher and your classmates to consider, too. In order to fully situate your writing, you may also want to consider that each topic has a sort of built-in readership that consists of those readers who are already interested in whatever the topic is and those who might be persuaded to become interested in the topic. Most topics and issues are already being discussed by people who are affected by the topic or issue. As you come up with topics for your writing projects, think about who might already be discussing the issue, what they might have already said, and what you might contribute to the "conversation." Too often, beginning writers write "in a vacuum," without thinking about how their writing could be part of an on-going conversation within a specific community of interested people.

In order to understand this idea fully, think about how you read. The first thing that you probably do is decide if you are interested in reading about the topic of whatever it is you are reading. Or, if you are not interested initially, you might find that the writer is beginning to make you interested by appealing to interests or values that you do have. If you find either of these to be true when you are reading, then you are part of the **ideal community of readers** for that piece of writing. The ideal community of readers for any writing consists of people who are already interested in the topic or who might be persuaded to become interested in the topic. If you think about the readers of your projects in this way, then you might begin to write with a real exigency and a real sense of readership. Then, classmates and teachers may evaluate your writing based on the readership that you are trying to reach, and this will produce a more effective learning experience for you. After all, the goal is not to learn how to write for teachers or classmates, but to learn to write for the various audiences that you'll encounter in the world outside of the classroom. Professional writers often use this idea of an ideal community of readers when they write because unless they specifically know who will be reading their work, they rely on the idea that their audience is already interested in the topic or wants to know more about it.

For every topic that you might consider writing about, there are, no doubt, those people who are not interested in the topic at all and who will probably never be interested. However, there will always be a group of readers who due to their experiences or values and concerns are already interested in the topic. There will also be those readers who might be persuaded to become interested in the topic if you can find a way to encourage their interest.

Writing for this ideal community of readers requires that you think in a more abstract way about your readership. When you write a letter or a report, you generally have an actual reader in mind. Writing for a larger audience of unknown readers—an ideal community of readers—requires that you imagine who they might be and what they might expect. Regardless of whom you are writing for, you should always ask questions about how to most effectively present your ideas to your audience. Writing for an ideal community of readers makes it even more important that exigency be taken into consideration by answering the following questions:

❏ What kind of readers might be interested in this topic?

❏ What might those readers expect from this kind of writing and what might they expect me to say about this topic?

❏ How can I most effectively address or challenge those expectations?

❏ How can I most effectively represent myself and my views in light of those expectations?

When you write for an ideal community of readers, you want to find ways to meet the expectations of those who are already interested in the topic in order to convince them to consider your particular perspective or to accept your explanations, arguments, or proposals. In the case of those who might be persuaded to become interested, you will want to find ways to encourage that interest and then to convince them to accept your perspective, explanations, arguments, or proposals. In short, before you begin to write, you need to do more than just come up with a topic and a thesis. You also need to create the situation for your writing by asking what you hope to accomplish, what your writing should look and sound like, who might be interested in reading about your topic, and how you can meet or challenge the expectations of those readers.

Answering these questions before you begin to write will also allow you to make other choices about the tone, language, format, and structure because these are all decisions that are linked to the readers' expectations. For instance, based on the topic, the genre, and the ideal community of readers that you have chosen, you can begin to answer more questions about the exigency for your writing project:

❏ What tone should I take in my writing?

❏ How formal should the language be?

❏ What kind of structures should I use to make my points? Should I tell a story? Provide facts and statistics? Will I need to explain some specific words and ideas to my ideal community of readers? How will I get my readers to accept my explanations, perspectives, arguments, or proposals?

? *Questions for Discussion:*

How have you thought about those who will read the essays you have written for your previous writing classes, and how does that differ from the idea of writing for an ideal community of readers? How do you reconcile the need to write "for a grade" in your writing classes and the need to learn to write for "real" readers?

THE IDEA OF DISCOURSE COMMUNITIES

Thinking about an ideal community of readers is one of the most difficult things for inexperienced writers to do. You may not have much experience with imagining how writing for the various types of readers can change the tone, language, and structures of your writing. However, you have lots of experience with adjusting your spoken language for various types of people you encounter and with whom you communicate, even though you may not have thought much about how or why you do that. If you do stop and think about it, though, you will realize that as you encounter various people and situations in your daily life, you enter into and pass through situations that call for you to make adjustments to the words you use, the way those words are spoken, and how you present yourself. This is not to say that our personalities change as we talk to different types of people, rather all of us adjust our language as we encounter various situations. For example, your level of formality will certainly change when you go from chatting with your family to talking with your friends to conversing with your teachers to discussions with your boss. You certainly would adjust the formality of your language for a job interview.

In order to understand this more clearly, it is useful to consider the concept of **discourse communities**, which is a term researchers use to indicate the various language groups that people encounter on a daily basis. The phrase "discourse community" refers to the ways people with a common interest have of communicating with each other. A discourse community, then, is a way of describing a group of people who share a particular way of using language, especially when they are speaking or writing about a certain subject or subjects. Some examples of discourse communities include those who play a particular online game or those who participate on an email list or a fan-site for a particular artist or musical group (see http://www.doomworld. com or http://halo.bungie.org for examples of on-line game community sites; see http://steveearle.net or http://www.lilkimzone.com for examples of fansites).

Discourse communities can be identified because the people who belong to them share a common interest and because they have words and phrases that are used in a specific way. As members of a discourse community communicate with other members, they try to make their language compatible with what the members of the discourse community expect.

The first place to look for an example of a discourse community to which you may already belong is to think about the way you use language with your family and friends. With these people, you have an enormous range of common experiences, a wealth of shared values, and a long history of previous conversations to draw upon. When you speak with family and friends, there is much less need to use formal language, to explain what you mean, or to consider what kinds of information they already have or might be interested in. In fact, you probably share lots of specific words and phrases that have a particular reference or meaning that you would have to explain to someone who was not well acquainted with your family and friends. You know this discourse community very well and participate in the special language uses without even realizing it. You know a great deal about what kinds of information they already have, you know a great deal about what values they hold and what their interests are, and you use certain words and phrases that have specific meanings within that discourse community.

Another way to understand this idea is to consider the discourse community of your chosen academic discipline (if you have chosen a major course of study) or the discourse communities of your city, state, or country. In the first case, people who are graduates of the various academic disciplines such as history, psychology, education, health, or business are all members of those discourse communities; they share a common way of using certain words and phrases and of presenting information. In fact, an important part of your college experience will be learning to speak and write using the language conventions of your academic discourse community. You will not learn to be a nurse, a teacher, a doctor, a lawyer, a systems analyst, a chemist, an accountant, a sportswriter, a business manager or a member of any profession merely by attending college and obtaining a degree. You will learn the basic tenets, theories, procedures, and skills to join your profession once you graduate, but you will also need actual experiences on the job. However, along with some basic knowledge about the discipline, the classes in your major area of study will teach you the discourse of your discipline. As you learn to use this discourse you become a part of the discourse community of that discipline. You will then know enough about how language is used in your discipline to take your place as a member of that discourse community.

Another way to understand this idea is to think about the way the citizens of this country form another discourse community. As you are aware, the United States is made up of an enormous variety of people with very different histories, beliefs, values, and even languages, but there are some values and ideas that most every American citizen is familiar with and that are very much "American," and these values and ideas are communicated to us and reinforced by the discourse that we share as Americans. "E Pluribus Unum," which is a motto that is found on some of our money, our official seals, and on some of our public buildings, is a Latin phrase that means "out of many, one" (see http://www.greatseal.com for a discussion of the motto as it appears on the Great Seal of the United States). This motto reinforces the idea that we all share in the discourse and the civic life of this country, even though our personal interests and backgrounds are varied. Interestingly, colleges and universities are an integral part of making sure that all American students are aware of the values and ideals we share as citizens. In effect, the introductory courses to history, literature, social sciences, math, and the sciences teach the basic introductory material and some of the discourse of that discipline, but they are also often designed to help teach the discourses of local, national, and global citizenship. Attending college teaches you the discourse you need to take your place within the professional and academic discourse community you have chosen to study, but it also teaches you to take your place within the various local, national, and global discourse communities to which you belong.

The idea of discourse communities should help you understand how the concept of the ideal community of readers works. As you imagine the ideal community of readers for your writing projects, think of what kind of expectations, values, and experiences those readers might share. They are interested in your topic, or could be encouraged to become interested in your topic, because they share some values and experiences. Your job is to appeal to those values in your writing. The idea of discourse communities should also help you reconcile the need to write for a grade with the need to learn to write beyond the classroom situation. In addition to evaluating how your projects address an ideal community of readers, your teacher will expect your projects to conform to the ways language is used and information is presented within the discourse community of academic writers. In other words, in addition to expecting that your writing will effectively address an ideal community of readers that is appropriate for your chosen topic, your teacher will also expect that, since the projects have been prepared as part of an academic writing course, your writing projects will look and sound appropriately "academic." Your projects should appeal to people within the discourse community of academic readers, and it should appeal to an ideal community of readers that is appropriate to the topic. To accomplish this, you will need to familiarize yourself with what academic readers value and expect, and consider what values and expectations the ideal community of readers for your particular topic might share.

A *Activity:*

Go to the website for your college or university and see if you can find your school's "mission statement." Read through the statement and examine how your school addresses the need to educate students to be "better citizens" of the state, the nation, and the globe. How do you think your school focuses on this part of its "mission?" As an alternative, you might also find websites for professional organizations in your academic discipline or chosen profession and examine how the "values" of this professional group are expressed in the specialized discourse on the website.

MAKING CHOICES ABOUT VALUES

Establishing exigency for your writing will be easier if you take the topic as an opportunity to consider a specific purpose for your writing and if you take that purpose as a point from which you can begin to think about writing for an ideal community of readers. Let us return again to our argument from the first chapter as an example. Our argument, after we adjusted it for stronger *ethos*, *pathos*, and *logos*, was:

> *According to a U.S. Department of Education survey conducted in 2003 and published on the website of the National Center for Education Statistics, 14 percent of American adults are illiterate. Tragically, this means that these people cannot follow the written directions of their doctors, figure out where to sign their name to an official form, or add up the simple numbers on a bank deposit slip. As such, we, as American college students, should consider volunteering in a local adult literacy program to make sure that all American adults are able to read and write.*

As we strengthened this passage, we chose to be specific about the readership and decided that the "we" that was to be addressed in our argument was "American college students." If we expect these readers to take action—to volunteer in a local adult literacy program—then we have to present a compelling argument that the problem of adult literacy in American exists, that college students should be concerned about it, and that they should invest some of their time in helping to "correct" that problem. One strategy is to imagine what possible values we might appeal to that this ideal community of readers might share. We can do this by asking the following questions:

❏ What kinds of readers might already be interested in this topic? What values, beliefs, and concerns might they share to which we can appeal in order to accomplish the purpose of our writing?

❏ What kinds of readers might be persuaded to develop an interest in this topic? What values, beliefs, and concerns might they share and to which we might appeal to heighten that interest?

If you look closely, you can see that some of these values are already built into the passage. The first sentence reads:

> *According to a U.S. Department of Education survey conducted in 2003 and published on the website of the National Center for Education Statistics, 14 percent of American adults are illiterate.*

First, the problem of illiteracy is constructed to emphasize that the problem is a national one. The statistic is not about global illiteracy (that would be a much larger percentage) but is specifically about the problem of adult illiteracy in this specific country. The statistic comes from the U.S. Department of Education and is published on a website sponsored by the National Center for Education Statistics (http://nces.ed.gov/). Already, you can see that the ideal community of readers that might be interested in this topic is the community of American citizens. We can hope that these readers will either already be interested in the topic of adult illiteracy in America or that they might be convinced to become interested in it.

The next sentence addresses some very specific values that this ideal community of readers might share. If you read closely, you will see that these values are included in the examples of what activities illiterate American adults cannot participate in:

> *Tragically, this means that these people cannot follow the written directions of their doctors, figure out where to sign their name to an official form, or add up the simple numbers on a bank deposit slip.*

These activities allude to some specific values that the ideal readership community of American citizens might share. These examples, which were taken directly from the Department of Education's report, are chosen to underscore very specific values.

The first example is that illiterate adults cannot "follow the written directions of their doctors." An ideal community of readers composed of adult American citizens might expect that other citizens should at least have access to a doctor, and that they should be able to take care of their own and their family's health. Mentioning this activity might also contribute to the emotional connection the reader might have to the problem of adult illiteracy. Many Americans might have an emotional response to this example—they might care that other citizens are able to take an active role in their own health care. Being able to go to the doctor and to follow the doctor's orders is a value that concerned American citizens might share.

The second example is that illiterate adults cannot "figure out where to sign their name to an official form." Signing official forms—voter registration forms, driver's license forms, lease agreements, work contracts, etc.—is something every American needs to be able to do to participate fully as a citizen. This is a value that an ideal community of readers composed of American citizens would also probably share. Being able to sign an official form is key to taking responsibility for yourself as a citizen.

The third example emphasizes the economic participation that this ideal community of readers might value and expect: illiterate adults cannot "add up the simple numbers on a bank deposit slip." American citizens might expect that other citizens will participate in the economy by holding jobs and supporting themselves. As such, the ideal community of readers might be interested in working on an issue (adult literacy) that supports this value.

All three of these examples have been chosen by the authors of the report because they appeal to some basic American values. Some readers might see these values as "rights" and some might see them as "responsibilities"; nevertheless, these are values that most American citizens will probably share to some degree.

In the argument we have constructed, the last sentence is designed to appeal to a specific portion of the discourse community of American citizens and to further define the ideal community of readers: the community of American college students. Although there are valid reasons why every American citizen should be concerned with the national adult illiteracy rate, the sentence specifically calls for "American college students" to take action:

> As such, we, as American college students, should consider volunteering in a local adult literacy program to make sure that all American adults are able to read and write.

As a subset of the discourse community of American citizens, American college students may be interested in this issue more than average Americans. We might assume that college students are developing a special appreciation for the value of literacy as a result of their academic studies, and that they may relate to the issue of *adult* literacy in particular, since most college students are in the process of reaching their own adulthood and are beginning to exercise their rights and responsibilities as citizens.

By choosing a specific ideal community of readers and by emphasizing values these readers might share, a rhetorically effective paragraph has been fashioned that includes carefully made choices about the appeals to credibility (*ethos*), emotions (*pathos*), and logic (*logos*). We have also indicated a specific exigency (the "tragic" situation of adult illiteracy in America) and established an ideal community of readers (the community of American college students). Additionally, we have attempted to address a system of values that this ideal community of readers might share.

As we have noted, thinking about the exigency for your writing may be a new idea for you. In your previous writing classes, you have probably engaged in prewriting activities that primarily helped you develop your topic; however, if you want to learn to write in ways that prepare you for the writing tasks you will encounter in your professional, civic, and academic careers, then you must do more than prewrite to develop your topic. Establishing an exigency for your writing before you begin to write that consciously addresses the issue of genre and readership requires that you engage in prewriting activities that help you establish an ideal community of readers and determine what kinds of expectations and values these readers might share.

 Opportunities for Writing

Make a list of some of the things you value. For example, do you value family, honesty, action, friendship, spirituality, etc? Pick one of those values and look up the word in the dictionary. Then, beginning with that dictionary description, write a paragraph about how you view that value and why you think it is important. Post that paragraph to your blog. You might also include an image or a group of images (either original or taken from other sources) that you believe also illustrates those values. For an interesting exercise in how images can portray values, you might go to Wikimedia Commons (http://commons.wikimedia.org/wiki/Main_Page) and type your "value" into the search box. What kinds of images come up? Note that Wikimedia Commons allows you to use their media, which includes photographs, drawings, video, and audio in your documents as long as you cite them.

UNDERSTANDING THE KEY CONCEPTS

1. To what does the term "exigency" refer in creating a piece of writing?

2. What is an ideal community of readers and how does that relate to writing an essay?

3. What is a discourse community?

4. How can a writer use the possibility of a shared set of values to persuade an ideal community of readers?

✓ Checklist of Questions for Establishing Exigency

1. What is the purpose for your writing project? What do you hope to accomplish?

2. What is the genre of the writing project? A letter? An email? An article? An essay?

3. What kind of readers will be interested in the topic of your writing project?

4. What might those readers expect from this kind of writing and what might they expect you to say about this topic?

5. How will you effectively address or challenge those expectations?

6. How will you represent yourself and your views in light of those expectations?

7. What tone will you use for your writing project? Serious, satiric, comic, etc.?

8. What level of language will you use in your writing project? More formal or more casual? Will you use any slang or contractions or specialized language for the discourse community of your ideal community of readers?

9. What values, beliefs, and concerns might those who are already interested in your topic share?

10. What kinds of readers might be persuaded to develop an interest in your topic? What values, beliefs, and concerns might they share?

11. What kind of structures will you use to make your points? Will you employ any narrative? Provide facts and statistics? Do you feel that you need to explain some things to the reader? How will these specific structures in your writing project contribute to the appeals of ethos, pathos, and logos and how will they help you make your points?

Blog Project

A "weblog," or "blog," is an on-line journal where writers generally post entries of their daily or weekly thoughts on their personal lives, the news, politics, their hobbies and interests, or on any other subject. If you are a member of a social network such as Facebook or MySpace on the Internet, then you probably have some experience with reading and posting to a blog. In the "blogosphere," there are, in addition to personal and social networking blogs, blogs sites that have been set up by individuals on politics, music, sports, fashion, travel, and just about anything else you can name.

In previous writing classes, you may have been required to keep a journal, or to turn in short, informal writings in which you explored possible topics for your formal essays, responded to readings, or just "warmed up" for your formal writing assignments. In this class, you will construct a blog that will serve these purposes. Generally, this kind of informal writing is not graded for "grammar" and correctness; however, you should keep in mind that other readers will be reading your blog. As such, you should make sure that the entries that you make to your blog are readable and contain only material that would be appropriate for a general academic readership.

Another way to think about this is to consider that, even though the writing you do for this class is safely stored away from access by just anyone, anything that you write on your blog should be something that you would not be afraid to stand up in class and read aloud (or have read aloud to the class by someone else). While the blog entries are not generally considered "formal" academic writing, these entries should adhere to the conventions of general public discourse: hate speech, excessive use of offensive language, intimate details of your personal life or the personal lives of others, attacks on individuals, slander, suicidal or homicidal thoughts, reports of illegal activities, inside information about your place of employment, and otherwise inappropriate and inconsiderate language should not be included in the entries you post to your blog.

Blogs are, of course, subject to the right of free speech; however, there are limits to free speech that are suggested either by a general sense of propriety (and in this case, classroom etiquette) and by certain legal restrictions, even in blog entries. If you are unsure of whether any of your entries might violate these limitations, ask a teacher or a trusted advisor. Each of the individual writing projects will require you to post entries to your blog, and the teacher may ask for other specific types of blog entries. You may also use the blog to develop the topics for your projects, to respond to peer review and the teacher's comments, to record personal thoughts about the readings from the chapters, and personal observations about what is going on in your life or in the world. As we have noted, though, be sure that your blog entries do not violate class etiquette, the usual bounds of propriety, or the constraints of good taste and common sense.

Setting Up Your Blog

Go to the *Choices* website and follow the directions for constructing your blog. Post a sample entry that describes a bit about who you are and the purpose of the blog, which will generally be to post required entries that relate to your writing class. In addition to the required entries, you are also encouraged to post voluntarily to your blog. In order to get a sense of what kinds of things bloggers do with their blogs, you should visit some blog sites on the web.

You can view some sample blogs by using specialized search engines on the Internet that search the "blogosphere" for blogs by subject, genre, or author. Currently, these include search engines such as "Blogdigger" (http://www.blogdigger.com), "Feedster" (http://www.feedster.com), and "Technorati" (http://www.technorati.com).

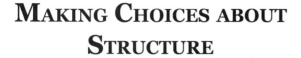

CHAPTER THREE

MAKING CHOICES ABOUT STRUCTURE

> "... the structure of a page of good prose is, analyzed logically, not something frozen but the vibrating of a bridge, which changes with every step one takes on it."
>
> --Robert Musil

STRUCTURES OF WRITING

Once you have chosen a topic for your writing project, worked to establish your ideal community of readers, and decided to what shared values you might appeal, you will still need to do more planning. Now you will need to decide how to support the main idea, thesis, or purpose of your writing. This supporting material could include:

- ❏ Relevant experiences that you or that others have had with the issue

- ❏ Facts, figures, and statistics from other sources

- ❏ The opinions and ideas of other reputable writers and thinkers

- ❏ Original analysis

- ❏ Original ideas, explanations, arguments, and proposals

- ❏ Appropriate charts and graphs, images, or video clips

As you can see, there are many ways to support the thesis of any writing project. You might begin by asking yourself what experiences and knowledge you already have about the topic and what experiences and knowledge your ideal community of readers might already have. While the tendency among many inexperienced writers is to immediately begin a web search for supporting information, it will help emphasize your personal perspective on the issue if you start with what you already know and what experiences you already have. Has anything happened to you that influences how you think about the topic? If so, then you might consider writing about that experience or those experiences. You might also be familiar with other people who have had experiences that might be pertinent, or you might remember things that you have read in the newspaper, in magazines, on the Internet describing other peoples' pertinent experiences. You might also consider including these experiences in your project. As you will see, personal experiences, either yours or others, can be very persuasive.

Next, you might ask yourself what you already know about the topic before you begin searching for support. Along with personal expertise on various subjects, each of us has a wealth of common knowledge about various subjects that we have gathered by watching the news, by reading, and just by generally paying attention to what is going on around us. This is called "common knowledge" and can be used to help support the main idea, thesis, or purpose of your writing project (see the supplement for research for a fuller explanation of common knowledge). Common knowledge most often needs to be checked against reputable sources, of course. Just because everyone says the same thing or believes that something happened or is true, does not make it so. Before you use any information you are not completely sure about, especially if it falls within the realm of common knowledge, you should check it against a reputable and reliable source.

In addition to what you already know from experience and common knowledge, you will then want to ask what new information you can gather to support your thesis or purpose. This is where you might begin to collect facts and statistics to support your argument. You might also consider collecting some ideas from other writers and thinkers to support your purpose. Chances are excellent that you are not the first writer to address whatever issue you are writing about, and the opinions and analysis and arguments of other writers may help you make your own argument. Be sure to read the supplement for conducting, collecting, and citing research before you begin to search for sources.

Gathering all this information—experiences, common knowledge, facts and statistics, and other people's ideas and opinions—is still not enough. Once you begin to sort through the varied types of support, you will need to analyze the information. After all, the reason your readers are reading your project is probably not because they are interested in what information you have collected. What they are interested in reading is what you think about all this information. How will your ideas, opinions, and research contribute to the on-going conversation about the issue? Writing a well-supported thesis means, then, that you need to know how to write about experiences, how to present and analyze information, and how to synthesize all this support into a coherent argument that takes its place within an on-going "conversation" about the issue. As such, you need to be comfortable with using structures that present stories and experiences—what we generally call **narrative structures**. You also need to be able to use structures that present and evaluate information—what we generally call **analytical structures**. In addition, you need to know how to employ structures that synthesize narrative and analysis into sound and believable explanations, arguments, or proposals—what we generally call **argumentative structures**.

As you are thinking about support for your thesis, keep in mind that computers now allow writers to control many elements of document design, so readers also expect that even unpublished documents will have a "professional" look. Writers today can easily add images, charts, graphs, and even audio and video clips as support and evidence for their arguments, so readers may reasonably expect that even student projects might contain some of these elements. Many teachers now encourage students to construct simple webpages and electronic portfolios to showcase their writing (as you will for this course), and so, increasingly, students are being taught to think of visual and even audio elements as an integral part of their writing. In fact, the same rhetorical concerns that we have discussed in previous chapters can be applied to visual elements such as images and graphics. When you consider what kinds of language you need for your projects, you may also want to consider how design elements may contribute, and you might want to consider adding charts, graphs, illustrations, pictures, or even short audio and video clips.

Choosing Narrative Structures—Why Stories Are Important

Generally, the word "narrative" is equivalent to the word "story." Narrative structures recount the writer's or another person's relevant and personal experiences as support for the thesis or argument. One way that you might use narrative structures is to help you communicate your credibility (*ethos*). Having had personal experience with an issue or being able to write about someone else's experiences creates a more believable position from which to present your analysis and argument. If readers know that some incident or event that supports your argument has actually happened to you or to someone else, then they may be more likely to accept your position as credible.

For instance, some of the most effective arguments against alcohol and drug abuse come from former alcoholics and addicts. The argument that drug addiction is a devastating disease with great costs to the addict and to those around the addict might be effectively made with facts and statistics that demonstrate the enormity of the problem, but the argument might be made more effectively if it includes the testimony of persons who have been through that devastation themselves. The effect of this kind of first-hand narrative is so compelling that authors have been known to exaggerate the extent of their addiction to heighten the drama of their stories (see http://www.thesmokinggun.com/archive/0104061jamesfrey1.html). News reporters frequently broadcast their stories directly from the scene to heighten their ethos. We are all familiar with shots of weathermen standing out in the wind and rain broadcasting the weather alert. What could they possibly hope to gain from this? The answer, of course, is *ethos*—credibility.

Writers may also use narrative structures about their own experiences or the experiences of others to provide logical evidence (*logos*) to support their arguments. One experience is not often enough to create overwhelming support of anything, though; nor would it generally be sufficient to cite even a few experiences as logical "proof" of anything. For example, it would be ineffective to argue that wearing seatbelts is dangerous just because a few people have received worse injuries when they were actually wearing them. In a preponderance of cases, wearing a seat belt has been shown to minimize injuries. Citing one, two, or even a half-dozen cases to the contrary is not going to convince most people to stop wearing seat belts. For every narrative that you could write wherein wearing seatbelts contributed to injuries, you could find hundreds of narratives wherein lives were saved by seatbelts. Still, narratives about or from people who were trapped by their seatbelts might be used to support the argument that seatbelt releases should work well. Although narratives are almost never sufficient "proof" of anything, they do demonstrate that something can or did happen at least once. Providing narratives of people who have had specific experiences can be one way of at least adding to the logic of your writing.

Narrative structures, then, may contribute to the credibility (*ethos*) and to the logic (*logos*) of your writing. Narrative structures can also increase the emotional appeal (*pathos*) of your argument. Stories about other people's experiences allow readers to empathize with those people and to imagine how they would feel if they were to have something similar happen to them. This is one reason why news reporters, when they report on a tornado or other natural disaster, interview individuals who have been through the disaster. Hearing from people who have lived through the event heightens our sense of emotional connection and increases the emotional appeal of the story.

Narrative structures, then, may contribute to the effectiveness of any piece of writing by:

❑ Strengthening the writer's credibility (*ethos*). Knowing that something relevant happened to the author or having the author relate stories about others who have had such experiences may make the author more credible.

❏ Providing logical evidence to support the writer's ideas (*logos*). Narrative structures may serve as evidence, although they are seldom adequate to provide the only evidence for any argument.

❏ Increasing the emotional content (*pathos*). Narrative structures contribute to the emotional appeal by offering the reader stories from people with which they may sympathize.

Writers sometimes create a narrative structure in which readers are asked to put themselves into a "hypothetical" situation or story. Creating these sorts of hypothetical situations can be another effective way to introduce narrative structures into your writing, although you should be careful to let the reader know that the experience you are describing is hypothetical. As long as it is clear what you are doing, asking your readers to imagine how they would feel or what they would do if something particular happened to them can be an effective way of getting your readers to think about an issue.

You should remember as you think about adding narratives to support your thesis, though, that narrative structures alone are seldom enough to provide enough evidence to support a thesis, unless the idea is one that can best be understood through a single individual's or a small group of peoples' experiences. When you choose to include narrative structures, make sure that the stories are appropriate to the topic, that they are representative of some valid point, and that they are remarkable enough to be interesting.

A ▸ *Activity*

Watch the local or national news and examine how news reporters make use of interviews with people to contribute to their news stories. Try to establish how these interviews contribute to the credibility, emotion, or logic of the report. You could create a video montage of various reporters covering the same news item. How do their various styles and approaches affect how the news story might be perceived?

MAKING CHOICES ABOUT DESCRIPTION

One of the most effective techniques to strengthen narrative structures is to make the description within the narrative as interesting, complete, and as "concrete" as possible. Narrative structures used in arguments are like other types of story-telling, such as those used by writers of short stories and novels, in that they contain elements of character, setting, and action. As with creative writing, in which stories are made up by the writer or "fictionalized" from actual events, the writer of non-fiction can also make narratives more interesting with vivid descriptions of the characters, the settings, and the dialogue.

Descriptions of the setting or the characters can also be made more convincing by employing specific details of the events. Even simple things such as the way colors are described can influence the reader's reaction. Perhaps the color of the walls in the room you are in now is yellow, but how would you describe that yellow color? Is it a dull, institutional yellow? A sunshine yellow? Is it as yellow as a young child's hair? Is it as yellow as the tobacco-stained teeth of your Uncle Ralph? Each of these descriptions of the color yellow would contribute to a different tone in the writing. As you are employing narrative structures in your projects, try to include appropriately vivid description. You might consider describing how things smelled, tasted, and felt, too. Inexperienced writers often begin and end their descriptions with how things looked; experienced and creative writers consider including descriptions that appeal to several senses.

Two other strategies that writers use to make their descriptive passages more vivid are **branding** and **dialogue**. "Branding" refers to using the specific names of things— the "brands"—to strengthen the description. What kind of car was the person in the narrative driving: a mud-covered Chevrolet pick-up, a brand-new Cadillac Escalade, or a dusty, broken-down Ford Escort? What kind of tree was it? A scraggly pine tree, a spreading oak tree, or a towering spruce? Using the specific names of things that appear in your narratives can strengthen the tone by providing more specific, "concrete," images. Concrete images help the reader imagine the scene as they are reading.

Dialogue can also strengthen the narrative, as readers will form more specific pictures of your characters when you use their words. In cases where the actual quotes of the people in the narrative are not of vital importance, writers will often "reconstruct" the dialogue to represent the actual words of the people in the narrative. If you are telling a story about what happened to you at home or in your fifth grade class, for example, it may be acceptable to reconstruct the dialogue as well as you can remember it. When you are quoting a real person, however, and the words of that person might affect their reputation, it is best to report what that person has actually said verbatim. In these cases, it is best to take notes on what the person has said or to use a recorder of some type. If you use a recorder, however, you should ask permission of the person you are recording first. To get a sense of how writers use dialogue and how dialogue is punctuated and paragraphed, it may be instructive to look in your favorite novel or in news reports to examine how experienced writers use dialogue.

The ability to employ detailed sensory data in your narrative structures requires that you develop a keen eye for detail and an ear for dialogue, and it requires the ability to transmit the desired impressions and tone to your readers. The idea is to recreate the experience through words in such a way that readers can almost feel as though they are experiencing the event for themselves. This is a skill that is not easily learned overnight, and creative writers study for years to be able to recreate scenes effectively. Nevertheless, with a little practice even inexperienced writers can improve their ability to write effective descriptive passages. Remember that the point of supplying vivid description and exciting dialogue is to create a dominant impression that contributes to the point of the writing. As you create your narrative structures, keep the following ideas in mind:

❑ Description should make use of all five senses, if appropriate. Try not to focus only on the visual components; consider including the senses of smell, touch, hearing, and taste.

❑ Description should make use of comparisons. Tell your reader what things look like, smell like, sound like, feel like, and taste like.

❑ Description should be dynamic. As the narrative progresses, the details may change as well. For instance, as the narrative reaches its conclusion, the descriptions might change or grow more intense.

❑ Description should focus on making a dominant impression. All of the descriptive elements should be employed to heighten the specific feelings and ideas you want your reader to have while reading your essay.

❑ Description should employ "branding" and dialogue.

 Opportunities for Writing:

Write a short paragraph describing the room you are currently in. Use vivid description, comparisons, and branding to create a specific tone that tells your reader how you feel about this room without ever overtly stating those feelings. Now write another short description of the room focusing on other elements and using other comparisons to create a different tone for the same situation. Post these paragraphs to your blog. As an alternate assignment, compose a video blog from your room using the camera in your computer or a hand-held video camera. In the blog entry, take us on a quick tour of your room concentrating on specific areas and items to create a specific tone.

Choosing Analytical Structures—What Does It Mean?

Bringing analytical structures into your writing might be difficult at first because analysis asks you to do two things you may not have much experience doing. Good analysis requires first that you examine your own thinking. Why do you think and feel the way that you do? What types of arguments and perspectives have you already accepted as you have formed your opinions? Second, good analysis asks that you make your thinking obvious to the reader. Readers generally want writers to supply more than just interesting stories or reports of what other people have said about an issue, and readers are looking for more than facts and statistics. Readers are also looking for some evidence of the writer's mind at work on the information, some analysis. That is the point of reading, really—to learn how a writer has synthesized and analyzed specific information. Readers will then decide for themselves whether they are persuaded by the writer's analysis.

Inexperienced writers sometimes react negatively to the whole idea of analysis. Is it not better to just present an accurate reporting of the information supporting an argument and then allow the reader to make up his or own mind? In fact, many people are suspicious of analysis; they may mistakenly believe that analysis involves looking "too deeply" for things that are not there. However, only inexperienced readers and writers will imagine that all it takes to persuade is facts and statistics, or that everyone will interpret the same set of facts and statistics in the same way. We all know that this does not happen, and that facts and statistics are always presented within a specific context that influences how we interpret them. That is the purpose of writing, really: to analyze the stories, facts, and ideas that you are presenting and to offer the reader your interpretation. This does not mean that the reader must or will accept your interpretation; it just means that you are offering your analysis for the reader's consideration.

Nevertheless, some people remain wary of including analysis in their arguments because they think it should be enough simply to present facts and statistics and then let readers make up their own minds. Of course, readers should, can, and will make up their own minds, but everyone relies on other people's analysis, and your readers will be reading your project because they want to know what you think. We all might like to think that we consider only facts and statistics to make our decisions, but we actually rely on other people to filter information for us and to provide quite a bit of analysis. If you watch various news sources on tv, you will see obvious examples. While they all report some of the same news, each of them focuses on different details and aspects of that news. Each one also offers "official" analysis, too. We are then free to make up our own minds about what we think, but we are certainly influenced by the presentation and analysis of the news sources that we watch. In reality, there is very little "pure" information that is not influenced by some analysis or by the context in which it is presented. As we noted in our own example of the statistic regarding adult literacy, even the way a statistic is reported can be a form of analysis (is it that 14% of adults are illiterate or that 86% of adults are literate?). At any rate, very few readers would want to read an entire writing project only to be told that they need to "make up their own mind" about the issue. Everyone knows that already. Even if the purpose of the writing project is primarily informative, readers will be interested in how the information in the writing supports the writer's specific point of view about the issue.

As you can surmise, then, there are ethical considerations in analysis and interpretation. Readers need to trust that you have been fair to the information you are analyzing. This means that your analysis must be based on interpretations that are supported by the information you are presenting. By the same token, though, it is perfectly permissible to present the information in a way that best supports your ideas and your analysis.

Analysis is generally done in two ways: either by "breaking down" the information into its component parts to see what it means or by grouping various pieces of information together to see what they "add up to." Simply put, analysis is taking pieces of information, statistics, and narratives and asking the question "so what?" Here are some things to remember as you begin to think about adding analytical structures to your writing:

❏ Even facts and statistics need to be analyzed and interpreted.

❏ Analysis and interpretation must be fair to the material being analyzed

❏ Analysis can mean breaking information down into its component parts to see what it means, or it can mean grouping various pieces of information together to make meaning.

❏ The purpose of analysis is to present your ideas about what the information means.

? *Questions for Discussion:*

What are your feelings about "over-analyzing" things? How would you describe the "right" amount of analysis? Can you give examples of instances where something has been "over-analyzed?"

A Sample Analysis

One of the problems that inexperienced writers have is in learning to use other sources for support. The first thing to realize is that the purpose of using sources is strictly to help you make your explanations, arguments, and proposals. You should never allow the sources to "take over" your writing; everything you bring into your writing needs your analysis. When you use information that is not original to you—whether that information is a story, a fact, a statistic, or an idea—make sure that you understand what that information means. That takes analysis. Let us imagine that we are interested in analyzing whether a passage from another writer on the subject of adult literacy will be useful for possible support of the argument we were constructing in earlier chapters. In order to find this passage, we searched our local college library using the search term "adult illiteracy." We then picked several books and articles and looked for passages that seemed to offer support for our argument. In a book entitled, *Adult Literacy: Issues for Policy and Practice*, by Hal Beder, we found the following passage:

> Illiteracy is a cultural phenomenon; the path to adult illiteracy begins at birth for the inner city and rural poor, blacks, Hispanics and other groups born into social disadvantage. For groups such as these there is a discontinuity between their culture of orientation and the social institutions of the dominant society. For them the values, social organization, and role relationships of the public schools are alien and alienating (147).

At first, it may seem that analyzing this passage presents a difficult task, but if we read closely with an eye toward **paraphrasing** the writer's main idea (putting the author's major idea into your own words), we might make a start. Working to paraphrase the main idea allows us to "crack open" the information to see what it means. More importantly, paraphrasing is the first step in applying original analysis. In order to come to a paraphrase, though, we need to break the passage down. In order to do that, we will look for four things:

1. **Patterns of repetition**: Look for words, phrases, and ideas that are repeated. Patterns and repeated words and phrases allow you to get a sense of what the important parts are. Simply making a list of the major words in the passage and grouping them into categories can help break the passage apart. Here is one example of such a list taken from the above passage:

illiteracy, adult illiteracy

cultural phenomenon, culture of orientation

path, begins at birth

inner city, rural poor, blacks, Hispanics, groups,

social disadvantage, social institutions, dominant society, social organization

discontinuity

disadvantage

values

role relationships

public schools

alien and alienating

Just by examining this list we might begin to get a sense of what the author is trying to say. You will notice that what dominates the list are words and phrases related to the ideas of culture, social institutions, specific groups of people, and values. So the passage is probably going to supply some kind of explanation of its first statement "Illiteracy is a cultural phenomenon," by linking illiteracy to the values people get from the social institutions and groups to which they belong.

2. Phrases and words that need to be defined: Look for words and phrases that need further definition, whether these are words that you need to look up in the dictionary or words and phrases that the author needs to define for his particular argument. What does the author mean by the phrase "cultural phenomenon?" How does that relate to the idea of "cultural orientation?" What are "social disadvantage" and "dominant society?" What is a "role relationship?" Does the passage suggest answers to these questions? One word that you might need to look up in a dictionary, even if you think you know what it means, is the word "discontinuity."

3. Places of ambiguity: Look for words and phrases that make you ask questions. What does the author mean by the phrase "the path to adult illiteracy begins at birth?" What does he mean by the phrase "alien and alienating?"

4. Binaries and oppositions: Look for places where the author sets one idea against another. There is one obvious place where the author sets up an opposition and that is where he writes about the "discontinuity between their culture of orientation and the social institutions of the dominant society." What is a "discontinuity" and what exactly does it stand between? What do you think that means?

A *Activity*

Using the list of things to look for in order to write a paraphrase, try to construct a one or two sentence paraphrase of Beder's passage above. Try not to quote more than two or three words of the original.

CITING YOUR SOURCES

When you use other sources in your projects, you will need to make sure that the reader knows that the information is not original to you. You will also need to let the reader know exactly where you obtained the information. In order to accomplish this, you will need to:

❏ Tell the reader where you obtained your information, citing the most important information about that source (which is usually the author's full name and the title of the book, article or website, and the page where the reader might find the information).

❏ Present the information from the source primarily in your own words (perhaps keeping a few of the author's words that might be particularly hard to paraphrase).

❏ Interpret the information for the reader by explaining what you think it means.

Let us see how all that might work in a paraphrase that we wrote:

> In his book, *Adult Literacy: Issues for Policy and Practice*, Hal Beder argues that adult illiteracy is largely due to cultural problems, especially for groups who are socially disadvantaged. Adult illiteracy, he writes, often affects this group because social institutions such as the school, which is where most people learn to read and write, have values that seem "alien and alienating" (147). Thus, people who are born into groups that are outside of mainstream culture have a harder time learning to read and write.

58

This paraphrase effectively presents some information that might be new to our ideal community of readers. More importantly, it expresses the new information in our voice—we have introduced the material, interpreted and analyzed the information, and told the reader what we think it means. See Supplement One for more information on paraphrasing, quoting, summarizing and on properly citing sources in your projects.

CHOOSING ARGUMENTATIVE STRUCTURES—SIGNIFICANCE, EVALUATION, AND PROPOSAL

In this more rhetorical approach to writing, we have often used the word "argument" to describe the purpose or thesis of any piece of writing. For our purposes, the word "argument" obviously takes on a much broader meaning than you are probably used to. You most likely think about the word "argument" in reference to two opposing sides going to war over competing ideas until one side "wins." In the rhetorical perspective, however, it will help if you expand your view of the word "argument" to include not just situations in which two opponents compete to see who can "prove" their point or until one side "wins." Here, the idea of presenting an argument also includes situations in which you merely try to persuade your readers to accept your particular perspective or explanation of a topic or when you ask them to consider taking some kind of action. The idea, once again, is that you are contributing to an on-going conversation—argument, if you will—about a specific issue. Think of your writing as a "mediation" into an on-going conversation.

A PROBLEM APPROACH TO ARGUMENT

One way to make more effective arguments is to address each topic as if it were a problem in need of a solution. Generally, writers who take the "problem approach" to their topics try to construct their arguments as answers to one or more of the following questions:

❏ Is this a significant problem that deserves our attention? In this form of problem-based argument, you might argue that something is or is not a significant problem.

❏ How big a problem is it? You can present an argument that something is a significant problem or that something that is perceived as a problem might not, in fact, be that big an issue.

❏ How did it get to be a problem? You might make an argument about how things got to be the way they are.

❏ What will happen if we do not address the problem? Here, you present an argument about the outcome of an issue if it is not addressed.

❏ What can be done about the problem? Here is where you might argue for a specific solution to a problem.

Several of these types of problem approaches can be combined in one argument, of course. In fact, let us see what we would need to emphasize in our argument about adult illiteracy if we were to take a "problem approach" in order to persuade our ideal community of readers that there is a problem, that the problem is significant, and that something needs to be done about the problem:

> *According to a U.S. Department of Education survey conducted in 2003 and published on the website of the National Center for Education Statistics, 14 percent of American adults are illiterate. Tragically, this means that these people cannot follow the written directions of their doctors, figure out where to sign their name to an official form, or add up the simple numbers on a bank deposit slip. As such, we, as American college students, should consider volunteering in a local adult literacy program to make sure that all American adults are able to read and write.*

Is this a significant problem that deserves our attention? How big a problem is it? If we are to persuade our readers that adult illiteracy is a problem that deserves their attention, then we must convince them that the statistic indicates that there is a problem. We might base an entire argument on convincing our ideal community of readers that 14% adult illiteracy is, in fact, a problem. In such a case, our job would be to provide stories, opinions, ideas, facts, and statistics that supported this argument. If we are going to ask our readers to be concerned enough to take action, we will also have to convince them that the problem is big enough to require action. That will also require that we convince our readers that the inability of 14% of American adults to complete these simple tasks is a large enough problem to warrant their involvement. This is what we have tried to do by emphasizing the values of American citizenship that these tasks represent. This argument would also need to be supported by stories, opinions, ideas, facts, and statistics. Finally, we will have to convince our readers that the action we are suggesting—volunteering at an adult literacy center—is likely to help. Thus, we would need to support the argument that our ideal community of readers needs to take the suggested action by using appropriate stories, opinions, ideas, facts, and statistics as support.

As you can see, these different ways of presenting arguments can build upon one another. You can argue that there is a problem, or you can argue that there is a problem and that it is significant, or you can argue that there is a problem, that it is significant, and that some specific action is called for. More information about the problem approach can be found on Purdue's On-line Writing Lab at http://owl.english.purdue.edu/owl/resource/588/01/.

CAUSE AND EFFECT

So far, we have used our argument about adult illiteracy to demonstrate various ways to use the problem approach to creating an argument. But we have skipped the question of how did adult literacy get to be a problem and what might happen if the issue is not addressed.

These issues point to another very specific type of argument that we might make about an issue: what caused or causes it and what are its effects? In cause and effect arguments, writers analyze why a problem exists, or they extrapolate that something that is happening now will cause something undesirable to happen later on. If you decide to make a cause and effect argument, remember that establishing cause or effect is often about probability rather than certainty. It may seem that something caused something else to happen or that something will contribute to a problem later on, but in order to deliver a convincing cause and effect argument, you will need to establish the "causal chain" for the proposition. In other words, you must show how the one thing did or will cause the other. Simply showing that one thing preceded another is not enough to show cause and effect. This is the way many popular misconceptions and even superstitions get started. You might have done well on a biology test when you had ham and eggs for breakfast, so every time you have a test after that you eat ham and eggs, hoping that you will, once again, do well. Are the two related? It could be that the increased protein helps you concentrate or improves your energy level, but the causal chain would have to be studied and established first. Although it may at first seem nonsensical that eating ham and eggs makes you perform better mentally, you might actually be able to make a convincing argument based on your own experience if you could find support from other sources that indicates that eating a high-protein breakfast improves brain function. There are many great sites on the Internet that can help you navigate the treacherous cause and effect argument. One great link is at http://www.literacymatters.org/content/text/cause.htm.

Examine the list of cause and effect arguments below and try to establish what kind of causal chains might be established to make an effective cause and effect argument:

1. Because of the Internet, people read less books than they used to.

2. Lowering the legal drinking age would cause more automobile accidents.

3. Michael Jordan changed the way basketball is played.

4. Video games cause school violence.

5. Sending another human to the moon will improve all our lives.

THE TOULMIN MODEL OF ARGUMENT

Another popular way to think about constructing arguments was created by Stephen Toulmin, noted philosopher and ethicist. Toulmin developed this popular model for constructing arguments because he wanted to give scientists, who might be more used to thinking of things theoretically, a practical way to solve problems.

To construct an argument using the Toulmin model, you generally begin by identifying the purpose or thesis of the argument. The purpose or thesis, as we have already discussed, is what you want the reader to think, feel, consider, or do after reading your argument. The purpose of the argument might be to convince the reader that something is true, or it might be to convince the reader merely to consider a different perspective. The purpose could be to convince the reader to actually do something. Whatever the end result of the argument is going to be, Toulmin logic labels that the **claim**. Returning once again to our adult literacy example, the claim of that argument might be that American college students should consider volunteering in an adult literacy program. As with the problem method, though, there are various claims that could be made about the issue of adult literacy. Our sample claim is, of course, only one possible response to the problem of adult literacy. Other claims might be that adult literacy is a problem in this country, that something specific is causing adult literacy, or that adult literacy is, in fact, a significant problem that needs a solution.

In this case, each of these various claims that could be made about adult literacy would be based on our statistic: 14% of adult Americans are illiterate by the Department of Education standards. In the Toulmin model of constructing arguments, this statistic would be called the **grounds** for the argument. The grounds for an argument, according to Toulmin method, are the basic data or demonstrable evidence on which the argument is based. As in the case of our adult literacy argument, some readers might challenge the Department of Education's definition of literacy or the way in which their survey was carried out, but most readers would be willing to at least accept that statistic as reasonable grounds to begin a discussion. If the grounds were challenged, though, the statistic itself would become a claim that had to be proved. Once it is reasonable to expect that readers will accept the general grounds for an argument, the writer can proceed to link the grounds to the claim through what is called the **warrants**.

Briefly, the warrants consist of the various arguments to ethos, pathos, and logos that link the grounds to the claim. These are the various methods of support that the writer uses to convince the reader that the claim should be accepted because of the grounds. In the case of our adult literacy argument, the warrants answer the question "why should the fact that 14% of adult Americans mean that college students should volunteer for adult literacy programs?" This might mean that the goal of the writer in this particular argument would be to convince the readers (American college students) that adult literacy is a big enough problem to warrant their attention, and that volunteering to work in an adult literacy program would make a significant enough difference to warrant their involvement.

So the claim is what you want the reader to agree to consider, to think, to feel, or to do after reading your project. The grounds are the basic premises, statistics, or evidence behind the argument, and the warrants are the reasons these basic premises, statistics, and pieces of evidence call for a specific response from the reader. Of course there may be details that need to be included about the warrants, and these are called the **backing**. If we used the warrants that adult literacy is a significant enough problem to deserve the attention of American college students and that adult literacy programs can make a difference, then the details we use to support those ideas would be the backing.

As we are considering how readers might respond to our argument, Toulmin suggests that we also consider adding **qualifiers** and **rebuttals**. Qualifiers and rebuttals are generally ways to limit the scope of the argument and to indicate the degree of certainty with which the writer presents the argument. Perhaps readers of our adult literacy project are already involved in other programs and volunteer work; perhaps there are no adult literacy programs in their area; perhaps some readers would consider supporting the cause of adult literacy in other ways. Qualifiers might be included in various parts of an argument in order to include positive responses from readers who do not completely agree with the grounds, the claim, the warrants, or the backing. Qualifiers are generally signaled by words such as "usually," "most" and "sometimes." Rebuttals are simply a way of thinking ahead to objections your readers might have and admitting that there may be some instances where the details of the argument do not completely apply. In the case of our adult literacy argument, we would probably need to consider that college students are incredibly busy. We might need to have a rebuttal that notes that although college students are incredibly busy, volunteering is at least something they should consider. Qualifiers and rebuttals are simply ways to indicate to the reader that the writer is willing to admit that the argument may not hold in all cases.

There is no question that using the Toulmin method to develop an argument takes some practice, but the results of using the Toulmin method to at least think about constructing an argument are always useful in planning a project. The basics of Toulmin methodology are:

- ❏ the **claim**—the purpose of your argument; what you want the reader to think, consider, feel, or do as a result of reading your argument.

- ❏ the **grounds**—the basic statistics, facts, or evidence that the reader needs to accept in order to respond positively to your claim.

- ❏ the **warrants**—the reasons why the grounds justifies the claim; the major supporting points of your argument.

- ❏ the **backing**—the details that make the warrants work.

- ❏ the **qualifiers** and **rebuttals**—the modifications and restrictions you put upon your claim and warrants.

If you are interested in learning more about the Toulmin model of argument, you might visit this site sponsored by Colorado State (http://changingminds.org/disciplines/argument/making_argument/toulmin.htm).

A ▸ *Activity*

Examine a short editorial from your local or school newspaper and see if you identify the argument's main claims, grounds, warrants, backing, qualifiers, rebuttals. Which of these elements do you find essential for an effective argument?

WHAT WE DO NOT ARGUE ABOUT

For our expanded notion of argument, it may be easier to describe what we do not argue about than to define all the possibilities for making arguments. By itself, the statistic that 14% of adult Americans are functionally illiterate does not present much opportunity for argument. It is simply a matter of measurement. Anything that can be demonstrated by simple means such as measurement is not, in itself, a cause for argument. You could argue with the Department of Education's definition of illiteracy or with the methods they used in their survey, but if you accept their definition and their statistic, then there is not much to argue about. Remember, though, that even facts and statistics need to be interpreted. Does the statistic indicate a problem or not? The measurement itself is not grounds for argument; however, what that measurement means, an analysis of the information, is grounds for argument.

Preferences are also not enough to create an effective argument. Suppose that you want to express your love of reading to support the argument, so you point out that "reading has changed your life." That statement may serve as an introduction to a narrative in which you describe your experiences with reading, but the fact that reading has made a positive impact on you does not necessarily support the argument beyond suggesting some positive *ethos* for you. The reader may simply respond: "So what? I hate to read and reading has never done anything for me. I've gotten much more out of listening to music and playing video games." Both of you have simply made statements based on preference that have come from your experiences. Just as there is no argument where the issue can simply be demonstrated to be true or false by measurement, there is also no argument where the issue is a matter of taste or preference based on experience.

Preference and matters of taste can, however, be explored to find out if there are grounds for argument. For example, is there anything at stake in someone not liking to read? Perhaps your personal analysis and research leads you to believe that people who do not like to read are at a disadvantage personally, professionally, and in their academic careers—that is a value that can be argued. You would first have to re-frame your preference for reading in terms that emphasized that value: "my experience and my research have led me to conclude that reading is necessary in a successful professional career." Now you have made a statement about value. Now there is something at stake. In order to proceed, you would have to define "necessary" and argue that reading meets that value. Generally, we do not argue about things that can be measured or issues of personal taste unless we can assign some meaning or value to those things. Until we do that, we do not have grounds for an argument.

THE PROBLEM OF OPINION

Even when statements are made in arguable terms, some may still believe that everything is just someone's "opinion." In a certain way, that makes sense. Everything that cannot be demonstrated by measurement or discounted as a matter of personal preference is, in a way, an opinion, is it not? Even after we analyze the information, interpret it, and assign some meaning or value to our argument it still may sound like a matter of personal preference, but don't be fooled by language. "Reading is necessary for a successful professional career" sounds like an opinion, but it is much more, since it contains an arguable value, which is signaled by the word "necessary." Because of that value, the writer is actually making an argument. Is reading necessary for a successful professional career or not? Just because something sounds like an opinion does not necessarily mean that we no longer have something to argue about—unless that opinion is really only a matter of preference or taste. One reason for this confusion is that we can attach "it is my opinion" or "I think that" to almost any statement, but attaching one of those phrases does not necessarily mean that the statement is simply a matter of personal taste or only someone's opinion.

A ▸ Activity

Examine the following list of statements. Which of those statements are merely matters of opinion, which are statements that can be demonstrated, and which opportunities for argument? Try to establish what value is present in the statements that can be argued and examine the matters of opinion to see if there is some value that can be added to them in order to make them into arguments:

1. I like the sport of football.

2. In my opinion, *Titanic* is the best movie ever made.

3. A football field is 100 yards long.

4. Mariah Carey's *The Emancipation of Mimi* is the best selling record of 2005.

5. I think that private ownership of assault rifles should be prohibited.

6. Everyone should become a vegetarian, in my opinion.

7. Smoking causes cancer.

8. I think that everyone should be concerned with global warming.

9. I ride my bicycle to school because it helps to save the environment.

10. Choosing a major in your freshman year is not necessary.

1. How does narrative contribute to the three appeals of an essay?

2. How can description be used to change the tone of an essay?

3. What are two ways to analyze a piece of information?

4. What is the "problem" approach to making an argument and how does it work?

5. What is the Toulmin method and how does it work?

6. Why are cause and effect arguments difficult to make?

7. What is the difference between a matter of opinion, something that can be demonstrated, and an argument?

✓ CHECKLIST OF QUESTIONS FOR STRUCTURE

1. Will you be employing narrative structures in your writing project? If so, will your narrative primarily contribute to the ethos, pathos, or logos of your project? How will your narrative accomplish that goal?

2. What particular descriptive methods will you use to make your narrative more vivid?

3. Do you anticipate using any sources in your writing project? Why?

4. Will you be applying a "problem" approach to the topic of your writing project? How? Will you be pointing out that there is a problem? That the problem is significant? Or, will you be supplying a cause and effect structure to identify the cause(s) of the problem or what effect the problem might have in the future?

5. Will you be using the Toulmin model to construct your argument? If so, have you identified the claims, the grounds and the warrants?

CHAPTER FOUR

MAKING INDIVIDUAL CHOICES: WRITING A LITERACY NARRATIVE

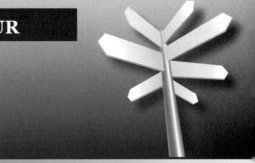

> "You can't make someone else's choices. You shouldn't let someone else make yours."
>
> --Colin Powell

THE SITUATION

When most people imagine the college classroom, they see rows of quiet students, seated at their desks and scribbling intently while the professor lectures: "In any right triangle, the square of the hypotenuse is equal to the square of the two sides"; "the causes of the Civil War were slavery, states' rights, and economic differences between the North and the South"; "the human body is 60-90% water by weight"; "the theme of *Hamlet* is the conflict between fate and free will;" "i before e, except after c." The students dutifully write down what the professor has said and then leave the class full of the knowledge that the professor has "deposited" into their brains.

The truth is that this popular idea of what happens in the classroom is based on several misconceptions about the educational process. One misconception is that learning is primarily a process of listening to lectures, writing the information down, memorizing it, and then repeating it on a test. Some of your classes may operate this way; however, the best education will not just try to "fill students up" with knowledge but will ask students to think about and apply what they have learned. The only way to accomplish that is to encourage students to combine the knowledge they get in class and from books with what they already know and to put that knowledge to work for themselves.

This is especially true in a writing class. The teacher might tell you what to write about, but the teacher cannot tell you what to write. While it is useful to take whatever writing assignment you have been given, apply what the teacher has said about the topic, and research what other writers and thinkers have said, you will, at some point, have to apply your own experiences, ideas, analysis, and thinking to the topic of your writing.

In order to approach a writing project in this way, it will help if you first believe and trust that your experiences, values, ideas, analysis, thinking, and words are meaningful in the classroom, and that you can use your prior knowledge and analytical capabilities to synthesize, understand, and even illuminate whatever the issue is in class. What good is knowing Pythagoras' Theory, the causes of the Civil War, the composition of the human body, the themes of *Hamlet*, or the rules of spelling unless you can apply this knowledge in your own life and work?

This kind of education requires that teachers do more than simply lecture, and it requires more of students than just taking notes and then regurgitating the information in papers or on tests. This kind of education requires teachers to value students' experiences and ideas, and it requires that students analyze and synthesize classroom knowledge to create their own ideas. This kind of education requires students to bring their own experiences and ideas to the classroom. This is especially true in the writing class.

A great deal of whatever writing ability you do have probably comes at least partially from the experiences that you have already had with writing. In fact, research has shown that two of the main predictors of reading and writing ability in any adult are how much reading and writing played a part in the home environment and how much practice at reading and writing the person received in school. If you grew up in a home where reading and writing were valued and practiced, and if you received good, quality education in reading and writing throughout your schooling, then the chances are greater that you have an appreciation for reading and writing and probably exhibit some skills at both. But do not despair if this is not the case for you. As we have said, anyone can learn to read and write well by applying some effort to the project of learning to do so.

Regardless of whether or not you feel you were privileged to grow up in an environment where literacy was valued, we believe that applying some analytical skills to examine these previous experiences with writing and reading can help steer your college writing career in the right direction. This project will ask you to write about your early experiences with reading and writing at home and at school. By examining what your attitudes are and how you came by them, you can begin to sort out just what language skills you have and why. Writing about your experiences may also encourage you to identify and begin to work on areas where you do have problems and to appreciate and rely more on the abilities you already have.

THE GENRE—THE LITERACY NARRATIVE

There are many accounts of how people have learned to read and write, and these stories are sometimes called **literacy narratives**. Many literacy narratives are powerful reminders of the importance of reading and writing to people's lives, and some of the most well-known and powerful come from those for whom reading and writing presented a way out of some dire circumstances. Take, for instance, one of the most famous passages in American literature, the recounting of how Frederick Douglass, a former slave, learned that reading and writing were the way out of slavery:

Very soon after I went to live with Mr. and Mrs. Auld, she very kindly commenced to teach me the A, B, C. After I had learned this, she assisted me in learning to spell words of three or four letters. Just at this point of my progress, Mr. Auld found out what was going on, and at once forbade Mrs. Auld to instruct me further, telling her, among other things, that it was unlawful, as well as unsafe, to teach a slave to read. To use his own words, further, he said, "If you give a nigger an inch, he will take an ell. A nigger should know nothing but to obey his master--to do as he is told to do. Learning would spoil the best nigger in the world. Now," said he, "if you teach that nigger (speaking of myself) how to read, there would be no keeping him. It would forever unfit him to be a slave. He would at once become unmanageable, and of no value to his master. As to himself, it could do him no good, but a great deal of harm. It would make him discontented and unhappy." These words sank deep into my heart, stirred up sentiments within that lay slumbering, and called into existence an entirely new train of thought. It was a new and special revelation, explaining dark and mysterious things, with which my youthful understanding had struggled, but struggled in vain. I now understood what had been to me a most perplexing difficulty--to wit, the white man's power to enslave the black man. It was a grand achievement, and I prized it highly. From that moment, I understood the pathway from slavery to freedom. It was just what I wanted, and I got it at a time when I the least expected it. Whilst I was saddened by the thought of losing the aid of my kind mistress, I was gladdened by the invaluable instruction which, by the merest accident, I had gained from my master. Though conscious of the difficulty of learning without a teacher, I set out with high hope, and a fixed purpose, at whatever cost of trouble, to learn how to read. The very decided manner with which he spoke, and strove to impress his wife with the evil consequences of giving me instruction, served to convince me that he was deeply sensible of the truths he was uttering. It gave me the best assurance that I might rely with the utmost confidence on the results which, he said, would flow from teaching me to read. What he most dreaded, that I most desired. What he most loved, that I most hated. That which to him was a great evil, to be carefully shunned, was to me a great good, to be diligently sought; and the argument which he so warmly urged, against my learning to read, only served to inspire me with a desire and determination to learn. In learning to read, I owe almost as much to the bitter opposition of my master, as to the kindly aid of my mistress. I acknowledge the benefit of both.

There can be no doubt of the importance of Douglass' early experiences to his future as a leader in the early civil rights movement. Douglass devoted the first part of his life to becoming literate, in spite of the fact that learning to read and write put him in grave danger. After gaining his freedom, he became one of the most gifted and famous speakers and writers in 19th century America. Of course Douglass did not achieve freedom, fame, and influence just by learning to read and write. The journey from slave to famous orator and writer required great bravery, much good fortune, and the help of many concerned and influential people. Still, it was Douglass' realization that literacy was the key to his freedom that set him on his path.

Not all writers recount experiences as powerful and as life-changing as Douglass', of course. Contemporary author Kurt Vonnegut couches his own literacy narrative in a slightly comedic tone, and offers the following advice for writers, which is based on his own experiences learning to write in school:

The writing style which is most natural to you is bound to echo the speech you heard when a child. English was the novelist Joseph Conrad's third language, and much that seems piquant in his use of English was no doubt colored by his first language, which was Polish. And lucky indeed is the writer who has grown up in Ireland, for the English spoken there is so amusing and musical. I myself grew up in Indianapolis, where common speech sounds like a band saw cutting galvanized tin, and employs a vocabulary as unornamental as a monkey wrench.

In some of the more remote hollows of Appalachia, children still grow up hearing songs and locutions of Elizabethan times. Yes, and many Americans grow up hearing a language other than English, or an English dialect a majority of Americans cannot understand.

All these varieties of speech are beautiful, just as the varieties of butterflies are beautiful. No matter what your first language, you should treasure it all your life. If it happens not to be standard English, and if it shows itself when you write standard English, the result is usually delightful, like a very pretty girl with one eye that is green and one that is blue.

I myself find that I trust my own writing most, and others seem to trust it most, too, when I sound most like a person from Indianapolis, which is what I am. What alternatives do I have? The one most vehemently recommended by teachers has no doubt been pressed on you, as well: to write like cultivated Englishmen of a century or more ago.

I used to be exasperated by such teachers, but I am no more. I understand now that all those antique essays and stories with which I was to compare my own work were not magnificent for their datedness or foreignness, but for saying precisely what their authors meant them to say. My teachers wished me to write accurately, always selecting the most effective words, and relating the words to one another unambiguously, rigidly, like parts of a machine. The teachers did not want to turn me into an Englishman after all. They hoped that I would become understandable--and therefore understood.

While the literacy narratives written by Douglass and Vonnegut are very different in tone and effect, they share the same topic: the importance of the author's early experiences with reading and writing on their futures. Significantly, in both pieces it is the author's analysis of the experiences that make them important for the reader. Simply telling the story is not enough. As we have pointed out, it is up to the author to give the experience its meaning by analyzing what it means.

THE IDEAL COMMUNITY OF READERS FOR THE LITERACY NARRATIVE

Remember that it is important not to simply write for the teacher or just to complete the assignment. You will also want to establish the situation, the exigency, for your literacy narrative, and to begin that process you should consider what sort of reader might be interested in reading your literacy narrative and what you want the reader to think, feel, or do after reading your project.

Almost every reader will share the commonality of having some experiences with learning to read and write, and some will be at least interested in how your experiences are different or similar to ones they may have had. In Douglass' narrative, we likely find little at first that is similar to our own modern experiences; however, Douglass just might convince us that if literacy is so powerful that it can make a slave completely unsuitable for slavery, then it can surely be a valuable tool in our lives. This is why Douglass' passage retains its power and relevance after more than a century.

Douglass' literacy narrative is effective at least partially because it has a strong *ethos*, because of who the author is. Douglass rose from the depths of slavery to become a respected writer and speaker. In addition, his narrative is delivered with a great deal of powerful description and detail. We hear his "master's" voice in dialogue that is made more potent through the use of realistic (if painful) language. His *pathos* is strong, and we sympathize with Douglass' position, even if we cannot fully relate to it. He carefully chooses his words to appeal to our emotions. The stark recounting of the master's words may trigger feelings of anger and revulsion, and he helps us to empathize by providing an analysis of his own feelings: the words of his master, he writes, "sank deep into my heart, stirred up sentiments within that lay slumbering."

The logic, or *logos*, of Douglass' narrative leads his literacy narrative to a startling and unusual conclusion. If learning to read makes a man unsuitable to be a slave, then Douglass will learn to read no matter what the consequences. That aspect of the logic is easy to follow. However, in the last sentence Douglass creates something new: he values the lessons in reading from his mistress—that we expect—but he also values the harsh lesson of his master; that we do not expect. The result is a very effective logical "twist."

Douglass constructs a narrative from his experience in which we, his ideal community of readers, are encouraged to accept the argument that literacy is a powerful force—not just for Douglass, but for us. His narrative appeals to an ideal community of readers who will most likely share the value of personal freedom, who will believe that he is a credible source of information, who will empathize with his situation, who will "follow" his logic to its unexpected conclusion, and who will accept his argument.

Whether you chose to focus your literacy narrative on your experiences at home, as Douglass does, or at school, as Vonnegut does, consciously choose how your own *ethos*, *pathos*, and *logos* will engage your interested readers or encourage your less-interested readers. Consider the details of your narrative and use them to strengthen the appeals.

THE TOPICS FOR THE LITERACY NARRATIVE

For the literacy narrative, you may want to start by examining your own feelings, ideas, and opinions about reading and writing. Do you love to write? Is writing something you use to express your thoughts or to help you clarify your personal choices? Or are you anxious when you have to write and rarely do so, even for yourself? Do you read for pleasure or only when you have to? Why do you think you have these attitudes and feelings? Is there an event or events that you can look back to that helped shape these feelings? Perhaps a teacher or a family member encouraged or discouraged you in your writing or reading. Perhaps you discovered a book or a favorite poet that inspired you to read more. Maybe you found that writing in a journal or creating your own poetry or songs helped you to sort out your feelings. It could be that you, like Douglass, found that literacy offered you a way out of a difficult situation. Possibly, like Vonnegut, you found that what you learned in school about writing or reading only made sense if you applied your own understanding to it. These are all possible topics for your literacy narrative.

THE PROBLEM APPROACH TO THE LITERACY NARRATIVE

One way to establish some possible topics for your literacy narrative is to apply the problem approach to making an argument. The following questions can be used to help you come up with a topic and with a structure for your argument.

❏ Is this a significant problem that deserves attention? Since you are writing about your experiences with reading and writing, it may be advantageous to decide whether you do, in fact, have significant problems with reading or writing. You might also focus on whether literacy is a problem in your community for many that you know and then offer your own story as an example of how and why literacy becomes a problem or how and why problems can be overcome.

❏ How big a problem is it? As you are thinking about your own experiences with reading and writing, you might want to examine the extent of the problem— either for yourself or generally. Was learning to read and write a big problem for you? Does your personal story about learning to read or write indicate a larger issue in our society in general?

❏ How did it get to be a problem? As you are examining your experiences with learning to read and write, make sure to show the causal chain. Just exactly how did those experiences influence you? What were you thinking when they happened or how do you think about those experiences now? What went on in your mind? Thinking about these questions will help you supply sufficient analysis for your narrative.

❏ What will happen if we fail to address the problem? Does your story suggest the results of these types of experiences for you? Is there something the reader might learn about literacy from reading your story that might suggest the need to address the issue of literacy in a larger context? If you suffered because of your experiences, what does that suggest about the possible effects of not addressing the problem of literacy effectively?

❏ What can be done about the problem? Does your narrative suggest some solutions to the literacy problem? For example, if your family showed a love of reading and writing, does that suggest that a possible answer to the problem of literacy in this country might be solved by getting families more involved? Does your story of an unbending or uninteresting teacher or class suggest something about how education might be improved?

As you can see, taking the problem approach to writing a literacy narrative encourages you think about how the reader might relate to your experiences and to think about your experiences in a way that suggests ideas for the reader. Applying the problem approach to the literacy narrative can be an effective way to make your narrative more than just a story. As always, the various elements of the problem approach can be combined.

THE TOULMIN METHOD AND THE LITERACY NARRATIVE

You might also consider applying the Toulmin method to constructing your literacy narrative. Here is one sample of how the Toulmin method might work in this case.

Suppose that the **claim** of your literacy narrative (the purpose for your argument) is this: having to read *The Grapes of Wrath* in summer school changed your mind about the value of being able to read well because it reminded you that you love to read and taught you that reading could be fun. The **grounds** (the basic facts) for that claim might be that being made to read a book in a classroom setting can, in fact, teach you something. The **warrants** for that claim (the major supporting points), would be the actual reasons that reading *The Grapes of Wrath* in summer school taught you that you loved to read and taught you that reading could be fun. The **backing** would be the details of those warrants. What exactly happened in your brain and in your life that allowed the book to teach you that? How, exactly, did reading the book teach you that reading could be fun? There could, of course, be **qualifiers** and **rebuttals**.

For instance, would the same book work for everyone? Would reading a book have the same effect on everyone? What other types of similar experiences might work?

This is only one example of applying the Toulmin method to your literacy narrative. Nevertheless, you can see how the Toulmin method can help you to clarify the claim of your literacy narrative and to emphasize the ways in which the elements of your literacy narrative work together to produce the claim.

POSSIBILITIES FOR NARRATIVE IN THE LITERACY NARRATIVE

Since the literacy narrative is, by definition, a narrative structure, it is important that you pay attention to the elements of "story" in your literacy narrative. Often, narratives begin in the middle of an important scene or at the point where the author realizes what the narrative means. You don't have to begin all the way back at the beginning of your life to write about an important moment. Whether you begin the story at its beginning or begin with your realization of what it means and then "flashback" to the beginning of the story, be sure to tell the reader near the beginning of your project what the point of the narrative is. In writing narratives, beginning authors sometimes make the mistake of just telling the story and relying on the reader to "figure out" what it means. Your job will be to construct some specific meaning for your story and to let the reader know what conclusion you have drawn from your experiences. The conclusion that you draw from your literacy narrative may actually serve as the thesis.

Remember that there is no requirement that you begin "at the beginning" of the story and proceed chronologically—skillful writers often employ flashbacks to "remember" what happened. If you do so, though, include transitional phrases to give the reader a sense of whether you are "in the present," or remembering what happened. Phrases such as "I remember when I was nine," or "later, I realized," or other transitions keep the reader from getting "lost" in your story.

Make sure to use concrete detail to convey a focused tone—serious, comic, ironic, etc.—and decide whether your language needs to be formal or more informal. Ask yourself how you can make your narrative contribute to your credibility as an author, how you can make your word choice contribute to the feelings you want your readers to have, and how you will use the narrative structure to make a point.

Narrative writers sometimes begin by writing the story first as a draft and then analyzing it to establish its meaning. You may want to begin focusing on the story and allow the meaning to become apparent to you as you write. Jot down whatever events come to mind as you think about your attitudes toward reading and writing and then plot them out, much as if you were writing a story that might become a screenplay for a film. Then, apply your analytical skills to establish connections between the event or events and your attitudes and feelings.

POSSIBILITIES FOR ANALYSIS IN THE LITERACY NARRATIVE

As you plan for your literacy narrative, keep in mind that your readers will expect you to analyze the narrative. As such, you might want to interrupt the story at appropriate times to indicate what these experiences mean to you. You do not need to be heavy-handed about this; notice that Douglass and Vonnegut skillfully inform us what they were thinking at the time of the event or what they realized after. Do not be afraid to add these interpretations as you write the story, but do not be alarmed if you find you need to write the entire story before you decide what it means. Once again, this is the beauty of written language. If you find that your analysis of the narrative is a bit "forced" or artificial sounding after the first draft, then you can "soften" it up. Or, if you find that you have not added enough analysis, then you can strengthen that aspect as you revise.

You may also want to include narratives about others to help you supply meaning for your literacy narrative. It might be useful to compare your own experiences with those of others or to locate other literacy narratives and make a comparison between your experiences and the experiences of others. Perhaps you can compare your feelings or experiences to those of a friend, a family member, or someone else from the time of the event. You could also supply some statistics or facts about literacy to help make the point of your narrative more clear to the reader.

If you do choose to include something that someone else has written, in this or any of your projects, make sure that it supports what you are saying and that you make use of your own analytical skills to show the reader how the words and ideas of others work with your words and ideas to make meaning for your writing. Never let material from other sources overwhelm your own words and ideas. Instructions for giving proper credit to another writer are contained in Appendix One.

POSSIBILITIES FOR ARGUMENT IN THE LITERACY NARRATIVE

Above all, try to make sure that there is a point to your literacy narrative. Writing that relies on narrative structures generally has an argument that is more nuanced and subtly made than traditional argument essays, but narratives still must have a point—in effect, an argument. Douglass' narrative argues that literacy could possibly set you free. Vonnegut's essay contains advice about how to overcome the problem of finding your "voice" in your writing. Both stories are presented as a way to make a point about the value of literacy. Constructing the argument for your literacy narrative using either the problem approach or the Toulmin method might help you establish whether there is something that your readers can learn about literacy from reading your narrative. The danger in writing narratives or narrative structures is that inexperienced writers are often satisfied with just the story. The meaning, the conclusions, the arguments that can be made from reading your story may be obvious to you, but readers will want to know, explicitly, what those meanings, conclusions, and arguments are.

A LITERACY NARRATIVE PROJECT

In this chapter, you were encouraged to examine the relationship between social, family, and school influences and your personal attitudes toward writing and reading. For this project, you will produce a literacy narrative, which is a recounting of the main experience or experiences that influenced your current feelings about the work of writing and/or reading. For some, these feelings about reading and writing may come from a time when they discovered a favorite author or a favorite book. For others, current attitudes about writing and reading may come from classroom experiences, good or bad, that occurred in grammar school or high school.

Perhaps a teacher encouraged or discouraged your interest in writing or reading. Perhaps you discovered that writing or reading took you to places where you could live out adventures from your imagination, or perhaps a family member's struggles or love of reading or writing influenced you.

As you begin to think about your literacy narrative, analyze your feelings about writing and reading and try to trace those feelings to a specific event or events that you can describe for your reader.

1. **Prewriting**: In chapter three, you learned how vivid descriptions of setting and characters helped the reader understand a narrative. Think about how you might describe the settings and characters in your narrative using concrete descriptions and "branding" to bring the settings and characters to life. You also learned how dialogue can help make the narrative more interesting. Complete a short passage for your blog from one of the following ideas:

   A. Describe a setting that you might use in your literacy narrative. Try to use "branding" and include as many senses as possible in your description (sight, sound, touch, smell, taste). Try to convey your feelings about that setting without directly telling the reader how you feel about it.

   B. Describe a character that you might use in your literacy narrative. Try to convey your feelings about this character without directly telling the reader how you feel.

   C. Write a short piece of dialogue that you might include in your literacy narrative and make a recording of it with different people taking the parts.

Listen closely to whether the dialogue you have written sounds authentic and adjust it accordingly. Pay special attention to what conflicts are being confronted in your dialogue. One of the best ways to learn how to write dialogue is to open a book that has dialogue and examine how the writer places the punctuation and establishes who is speaking.

2. **Drafting**: After you have come up with a possible storyline for your literacy narrative, complete the Checklist of Questions of Establishing Exigency (p.44) and the Checklist of Questions for Structure (p.67). Read some of your classmates' blogs on this issue and consider what made their blog posts work well or what they might have done better. Plot the chronology of the narrative carefully before you begin. Will you have flashbacks or will your story proceed chronologically? As always, carefully consider what you will analyze in your essay and what you will argue about.

   Narrative: Since this project is about you, your experiences, and how those experiences formed your attitudes about literacy, make sure to provide more than just a description of the events. It is also important to interrupt the narrative with analysis so that your narrative has a point.

   Analysis: The connections between the events you are describing in your literacy narrative and your feelings about writing and/or reading are important to the success of this project. In effect, you are analyzing these events to suggest how they caused you to feel a certain way.

   Argument: In this project, you are arguing for your particular interpretation of your experiences. The goal is to convince the reader that your feelings about writing and/or reading are justified by the events. Consider why the reader would believe in your interpretation of these events, how the description and the story might help persuade the reader that you are justified in your attitudes, and what emotion or emotions you might want the reader to feel as he or she reads your literacy narrative.

3. **Peer Review**: After you complete the first draft, send it to your peer review group for review and complete your reviews of their first drafts using the peer review questionnaire for this project (located on the next page or in the online Choices Portal).

4. **The Visual**: Select an appropriate visual image to accompany your literacy narrative and complete the Checklist for Visuals (p. 204). If your narrative

focuses on your family life, you might consider using a picture or a group of pictures of your family engaged in a typical activity. If your narrative focuses on something that happened to you in school, you might consider using a picture of your school or the school emblem. If your narrative focuses on a favorite book or author, you might consider using a picture of that book or that author.

5. **Revision and Proofing**: After you have selected your visual, completed your peer reviews, and received your peer-review responses, make revisions and check your sentences. Check your work against the Checklist of Questions for Process (p. 27). As always, you will want to read your final draft aloud before you consider it complete. Follow the instructions for uploading project one.

Peer Review Questionnaire for the Literacy Narrative

Your Name:

Title of the project you are peer reviewing:

Author of the project:

Answer the following questions about the project you are reviewing in a complete sentence or in a short paragraph.

1. Summarize what you take from the project to be the writer's main attitude toward reading and/or writing:

2. Describe what you like most about the project you are reviewing:

3. Find a sentence that contains the most vivid description of setting or character and copy that sentence here:

4. If the writer were to add anything else to the project, what would you suggest adding: more description, more analysis, a stronger introduction or conclusion? Be as specific as you can:

5. Is there anyplace in the literacy narrative where the writer tends to wander off topic or loses the focus of the project? Be as specific as you can:

6. If the writer has included a visual image with the project, how do you think the visual adds to the project? Does it seem appropriate to the project? Does it contribute to the project? How? Could you suggest a more useful or appropriate visual for the project?

CHAPTER FIVE

MAKING COMMUNITY CHOICES: WRITING THE INFORMED OPINION

> "Democracy cannot succeed unless those who express their choice are prepared to choose wisely. The real safeguard of democracy, therefore, is education."
>
> --Franklin D. Roosevelt

THE SITUATION

You may have heard of the game "six degrees of Kevin Bacon," in which players try to connect a randomly chosen actor to the actor Kevin Bacon. The connection is made by tracking the chosen actor to another actor by a movie both were in, and then connecting the other actor to another until you arrive at an actor who was in a film with Kevin Bacon. Supposedly, almost any actor can be connected to Kevin Bacon by less than six "moves." In fact, Kevin Bacon has been in so many films that it is difficult to name any well-known actor that cannot be linked to Bacon in more than two "moves." You can visit a website created at the University of Virginia that demonstrates this phenomenon (http://oracleofbacon.org/).

This is more than just a game, however. Scientists have tried to prove the hypothesis, which did not originate with the Kevin Bacon game, that any two people on the planet can be connected by less than six other people. Although the theory remains unproven, primarily because the ability to connect people depends so much on factors such as their economic status, researchers agree that the more any two people have in common, the easier it is to show how they are connected. Kevin Bacon is easily connected to almost any chosen actor because both Bacon and the actor share the commonality of appearing in movies. Likewise, mathematicians, musicians, people who watch the same types of movies, chess players, fans of the Buffalo Bills, and people who have pages on Facebook or MySpace can likely be connected in a few "moves" because they share that common interest.

What the game suggests is that it is, as the saying goes, a small world. In fact, early work on this theory was called the "small world problem." What is obvious is that the more you participate in different kinds of activities, the more likely you are to be linked with a larger number of people. If you introduce commonalities then you greatly increase the chances of any two people being linked. Once you accept that you are linked to millions of others by various commonalities, it may become easier to believe that your actions affect the lives of others and that others' actions have an effect on you.

The point of all this is that your potential to be heard and to affect the communities in which you live is probably greater than you might imagine. Most significant change, in fact, can be traced to an individual who suggested the right solution to a problem at the right time, who complained about an injustice when no one was willing to, or who was willing to be the first to take action. For example, most historians date the beginning of the modern civil rights movement to the actions of Rosa Parks, a black woman who, in 1955, refused to give up her seat on a bus to a white passenger, even though a city ordinance required her to do so. While most of us will not be called upon to be as brave as Rosa Parks, we can at least speak up about the issues in our communities that matter to us.

At first, the word "community" may conjure up images of small-town America— white picket fences, quaint churches, local festivals and improvement projects, backyard cookouts, and local clubs and coffeehouses. Sometimes, people imagine that American communities were stronger in "the good old days," when people knew their neighbors, doors were unlocked, and crime, poverty, hunger, disease, and environmental degradation were big city problems. The temptation is to look at reruns of 1950's and 60's television shows like *Andy Griffith* or *Leave It to Beaver* as accurate portrayals of American life as it used to be, but these slice-of-life visions of the "good old days" are largely fictional. For some, the 50's and 60's may have been a less complicated time, but that is probably because injustices and inequities allowed some people to insulate themselves from the problems that others in the world faced daily. Crime, poverty, hunger, disease, and environmental problems were just as real in those days, but economic and class status allowed some people to escape those problems. Now, the pervasive nature of these issues and the ability to communicate and travel more easily has brought these problems to everyone's door; in fact, it is probably true that the distance that many felt from the problems of the world in the "good old days" only helped to make the problems worse. The good news is that the interconnectedness that makes these serious problems more universal and more apparent to all of us also allows for more voices to be heard, more solutions to be offered, and more individual action. Just as Rosa Park's refusal to give up her seat helped start a movement that changed the entire American landscape, so can any individual be heard on the important issues that we all face.

Take the issue of recycling. There are indubitably millions of people who are interested in recycling, although the range of ideas and opinions are varied. Nevertheless, you will probably find that some local group shares an interest in recycling and that local group is connected to a national group. By mapping out these communities you may begin to realize that the possibility of one voice being heard is greater than might first be imagined. If you were to think of an innovation in how things are recycled or suggest a way to promote more recycling in your community, you might affect the lives of countless people as this idea could spread through the interconnected system of the community of people who are interested in recycling issues.

THE GENRE—THE INFORMED OPINION

So where do you have the chance to express your informed opinions to your community? Where would a writing project about a community issue most likely appear? The most obvious answer might be on the editorial page of your local or school newspaper. Writing a letter to the editor or a guest editorial could give you the opportunity to express your views on community, national, or world issues in a way that might influence or persuade others. If your issue concerns a more specific community, then you might investigate writing an opinion piece or a letter to a publication that is targeted to that community. There are blogs and forums that invite contributions on issues of relevance to the readers, and many local and national groups have newsletters to which readers may contribute essays and letters. Many newspapers, magazines, newsletters, and blogs take contributions from readers. One source of publication for writers are "zines," which is short for "fanzines." These are low-budget publications that are published away from the mainstream media and that offer more space for writers to publish their views and ideas on a variety of subjects. Letters to local or national officials are another genre of community writing that can have results, as are pamphlets and posters that present ideas about issues.

You may have difficulty imagining that you have anything worthwhile to say about issues that affect your school or the various communities to which you belong. Still, as a tuition-paying student; as a person with varied interests; as a tax-paying voter of your city, county, state and nation; and as a citizen of the world you do have the right—perhaps even the responsibility—to voice your opinions. The difference between offering just an opinion—and we know now that even opinions are a form of argument—and an informed opinion are that the informed opinion is just that: an argument based on *logos*, *ethos*, and *pathos*. In this case, the word "opinion" indicates the genre of the argument and not just that the argument is merely your opinion. Perhaps you feel that your expertise is not yet what it should be to contribute your informed opinion to these discussions; however, you should know that the best ideas often come from those who are not highly trained or experienced. This is true because people who are not too close to the issue see solutions that those who are "inside" the issue have overlooked. Whether you believe you have the knowledge or experience to contribute effectively, you can at least practice the writing skills that will allow you, once you do feel more confident about your ability to contribute, to become an eventual voice in these discussions.

Let us take a look at two different pieces of community writing. The first is an editorial from journalist Ross Gelbspan, entitled "Katrina's Real Name." This editorial appeared in *The Boston Globe* on August 30, 2005—one day after hurricane Katrina devastated the Gulf Coast:

> *The Hurricane that struck Louisiana yesterday was nicknamed Katrina by the National Weather Service. Its real name is global warming.*
>
> *When the year began with a two-foot snowfall in Los Angeles, the cause was global warming.*
>
> *When 124-mile-an-hour winds shut down nuclear plants in Scandinavia and cut power to hundreds of thousands of people in Ireland and the United Kingdom, the driver was global warming.*
>
> *When a severe drought in the Midwest dropped water levels in the Missouri River to their lowest on record earlier this summer, the reason was global warming.*
>
> *In July, when the worst drought on record triggered wildfires in Spain and Portugal and left water levels in France at their lowest in 30 years, the explanation was global warming.*
>
> *When a lethal heat wave in Arizona kept temperatures above 110 degrees and killed more than 20 people in one week, the culprit was global warming.*
>
> *And when the Indian city of Bombay (Mumbai) received 37 inches of rain in one day--killing 1,000 people and disrupting the lives of 20 million others--the villain was global warming.*
>
> *As the atmosphere warms, it generates longer droughts, more-intense downpours, more-frequent heat waves, and more-severe storms.*

Although Katrina began as a relatively small hurricane that glanced off south Florida, it was supercharged with extraordinary intensity by the relatively blistering sea surface temperatures in the Gulf of Mexico.

The consequences are as heartbreaking as they are terrifying.

Unfortunately, very few people in America know the real name of Hurricane Katrina because the coal and oil industries have spent millions of dollars to keep the public in doubt about the issue.

The reason is simple: To allow the climate to stabilize requires humanity to cut its use of coal and oil by 70 percent. That, of course, threatens the survival of one of the largest commercial enterprises in history.

In 1995, public utility hearings in Minnesota found that the coal industry had paid more than $1 million to four scientists who were public dissenters on global warming. And ExxonMobil has spent more than $13 million since 1998 on an anti-global warming public relations and lobbying campaign.

In 2000, big oil and big coal scored their biggest electoral victory yet when President George W. Bush was elected president--and subsequently took suggestions from the industry for his climate and energy policies.

As the pace of climate change accelerates, many researchers fear we have already entered a period of irreversible runaway climate change.

Against this background, the ignorance of the American public about global warming stands out as an indictment of the US media.

When the US press has bothered to cover the subject of global warming, it has focused almost exclusively on its political and diplomatic aspects and not on what the warming is doing to our agriculture, water supplies, plant and animal life, public health, and weather.

For years, the fossil fuel industry has lobbied the media to accord the same weight to a handful of global warming skeptics that it accords the findings of the Intergovernmental Panel on Climate Change--more than 2,000 scientists from 100 countries reporting to the United Nations.

Today, with the science having become even more robust--and the impacts as visible as the megastorm that covered much of the Gulf of Mexico--the press bears a share of the guilt for our self-induced destruction with the oil and coal industries.

As a Bostonian, I am afraid that the coming winter will--like last winter--be unusually short and devastatingly severe. At the beginning of 2005, a deadly ice storm knocked out power to thousands of people in New England and dropped a record-setting 42.2 inches of snow on Boston.

The conventional name of the month was January. Its real name is global warming.

Notice that Gelbspan begins his editorial with the startling thesis that Hurricane Katrina was made more devastating by global warming. He then builds a sense of urgency into his argument with a serious of sentences that build through repetition and similar rhythm. Each of the paragraphs that follows the short introduction is a single sentence that begins with the same phrase, and each sets up a cause and effect argument linking weather abnormalities to global warming. Cause and effect arguments require causal connections, and Gelbspan attempts to provide those causal connections in two more single-sentence paragraphs—first the general link from atmospheric warming to general weather changes, and then the link from atmospheric warming specifically to hurricane Katrina.

The style of the editorial—brief paragraphs, very little introduction, and succinct argument—is what readers' expect from the genre of the newspaper editorial. Journalists know that readers of the editorial page want brief arguments and lots of easily understood support. Notice then, how Gelbspan attempts to strengthen his argument by introducing an emotional appeal through the use of carefully chosen emotionally charged words: "The consequences are as heartbreaking as they are terrifying."

Next come Gelbspan's indictments of the government for failing to recognize the dangers of global warming and for undermining its acceptance as a real problem. Gelbspan also accuses the media of failing to report the issue adequately. Embedded in this argument is a subtle call for readers to educate themselves about the subject and, perhaps, to take action. Whether you believe that the argument is successful or not, notice how the genre of the newspaper editorial can be used to suggest action.

Now let us look at a different sort of presentation; this time from a website sponsored by a student environmental group at the University of Oregon:

Almost everything creates waste. According to the US Environmental Protection Agency: "In 1999, U.S. residents, businesses, and institutions produced more than 230 million tons of MSW, which is approximately 4.6 pounds of waste per person per day, up from 2.7 pounds per person per day in 1960" (www.epa.gov). Traditionally, most garbage is buried in landfills. But landfills are filling up and closing down all over the country. In 1986, there were 7,683 municipal solid waste landfills. A survey done in 1995, showed only 3,581.

Incineration is a poor alternative. According to The Recycler's Handbook (Earthworks Group 1990): "Even with pollution controls, incinerators are the largest new source of air pollution in most communities. They spew out gases that contribute to acid rain. These gases include up to 27 toxic heavy metals, acid gases, carbon monoxide and dioxins. Additionally, incinerators produce millions of tons of toxic ash, which still have to go to landfills."

In The Solid Waste Dilemma, An Agenda for Action published by the EPA/530-SW-89-019 in 1989, integrated waste management was referred to as "the complementary use of a variety of waste management practices to safely and effectively handle the municipal solid waste stream with the least adverse impact on human health and the environment."

When deciding how to handle solid waste, consider the alternatives in this order: source reduction (includes reuse), recycling, incineration, then land filling. This hierarchy has remained unchanged and is still regarded as the best way to handle solid waste.

Source reduction, the highest goal in the solid waste management hierarchy, should be the centerpiece of every business or government procurement program. Source reduction is first in the solid waste hierarchy. Although recycling questions and changes how products are manufactured, it is not designed to question why they are produced. Source reduction asks those questions: Do we need this? If so, can it be produced with fewer resources, take up less space or make a lighter environmental impact? A "source reduction product" can be defined as "a product that results in a net reduction in the generation of waste compared to the previous or alternate version and includes durable, reusable and remanufactured products; products with no or reduced

toxic constituents; and products marked with no or reduced packaging."

Sometimes source reduction comes from the product itself, e.g. lighter product packaging. Other times, it has more to do with how the product is used. Sometimes buying for source reduction means that several different parts of an organization must agree on policies that result in fewer or different products being purchased. It's time to think before buying and reduce the amount of overall waste produced in the first place. This is called Precycling. It is a choice to make when shopping.

Reusing starts at the point of purchase. Choose products that can be maintained and repaired to ensure a longer life.

Recycling, as the word indicates, is a cyclical process. After purchasing a product and using it to its full potential, a choice becomes evident: Throw it away or recycle it. If there is an available market choose recycling. According to the University of Oregon Factoids Section:

❏ *Every year enough energy is saved by recycling steel to supply L.A. with nearly a decade's worth of electricity.*

❏ *Making one ton of recycled paper uses only about 60% of the energy needed to make a ton of virgin paper.*

❏ *Every aluminum can that is recycled saves 95 percent of the energy that it would have taken to manufacture a new one from bauxite. In other words, when a can is tossed in the trash as much energy is thrown away as if the can was half full of gasoline. Recycling one aluminum can run a TV for three hours.*

❏ *Recycling glass lowers the melting point for the new glass, saving up to 32% of the energy needed for production.*

❏ *Recycling reduces dependence on landfills and incinerators.*

❏ *Every year Americans throw away nearly 10 million tons of newspaper. If these papers were all recycled, over 150 million trees would be left standing, less than half as much energy would be used, and air pollution from the manufacturing process would be cut by more than 70 percent.*

❏ *America imports most of its oil. Saving energy by recycling means we depend less on foreign supplies and reduce environmental problems such as global warming, acid rain and oil spills directly linked to our energy use.*

Recycling reduces the amount of pollution created during the manufacturing process. The end result is cleaner air, land, and water. The earth's resources are finite. Reduce, reuse or recycle to conserve valuable resources.

In order for recycling to be successful, there must be a demand for use of recycled materials. Colleges have a unique opportunity to demand products: made with reduced and recyclable packaging, made with recycled content and made to last, while being repairable for the long haul.

Colleges and Universities are educating future leaders. Day-to-day operations serve as an example to students and the greater community. Using resources efficiently and effectively, collecting materials for recycling and purchasing non-toxic recycled content products will enhance the reputation of the school, while reducing costs and contributing to a better world.

Just as Gelbspan does in his editorial, the authors of this website employ facts and statistics to support their argument. However, notice the difference in the presentation in the genre of a news editorial and in the genre of a website. In the editorial, the emphasis is on making the argument quickly and relying on common knowledge and opinion. The website, on the other hand, cites the sources for many of its facts and statistics.

Notice also the image that the students have used. At first, we might question how the image supports the argument; however, it may help bring a personal touch to what might be a fairly "dry" topic. The image reminds us that there are real people behind the push for recycling and precycling at the university.

A ▶ *Activity*:

Gather into small groups and discuss the examples above in more detail. How do the genre, the intended readership, and the subject change the presentation of the argument?

THE IDEAL COMMUNITY OF READERS FOR COMMUNITY WRITING

When making arguments about community issues, it is essential to identify your ideal community of readers. Unless you consider what that ideal community of readers might already know about an issue and what arguments they have already heard and made up their minds about, you risk repeating information that your readers already know or you risk simply "rehashing" arguments that your readers have already accepted or rejected. In other words, to make a successful appeal to *logos* on a community issue, you need to present new information, make new connections, or suggest some action that your ideal community of readers may not have considered. For example, in the editorial, Gelbspan emphasizes connections between global warming and recent natural disasters that readers may not have considered before. On the webpage, the focus is on providing statistics, new definitions, and new courses of action. Readers are likely to have heard about global warming and recycling, but Gelbspan attempts to make new connections between specific weather events and the issue of global warming. Readers of the student website are likely to be familiar with most of the arguments in favor of recycling, but the student website provides statistics that all readers may not be familiar with and presents a new alternative to recycling: "precycling."

Unless you are asking your readers to consider an issue that they have not heard much about, they have probably already considered many of the standard arguments about most community-related issues. For instance, many students try to write community-based arguments on abortion, gun control, or the legalization of marijuana. Most people have already heard the basic arguments on all sides of these subjects, and unless you can provide some new information or suggest some new course of action, you will likely be repeating arguments that most readers have already either rejected or accepted.

To avoid this mistake, you can use these categories to design your argument for your ideal community of readers:

1. Readers who do not know about the issue or who are not familiar enough with it to realize that it is a significant problem. In this case, supply information and make connections to inform readers of the problem and to persuade them that it is serious enough to warrant their attention.

2. Readers who most likely agree or are leaning toward agreement with you on the issue. In this case, think about what arguments readers have probably already accepted to avoid "preaching to the choir." Instead, supply new information, make new connections, or suggest a course of action that readers may not have considered before.

3. Readers who most likely disagree or are leaning toward disagreement with you on the issue. In this case, consider what arguments readers have already rejected and avoid simply repeating old and familiar arguments. Instead, ask yourself if you can make an argument that readers may not have heard, or if you can make a familiar argument more persuasive by supplying new information or making new connections.

Deciding where your essay might appear—in a newspaper, in a newsletter, or on a blog, for instance—will help you identify the ideal community of readers. Each of these possible "sites" for your writing already has a "built-in" community of readers. For example, readers of a newsletter or blog published by an environmental group will already have heard and agreed with most of the arguments in favor of recycling; the readers of a newspaper's editorial page will have more varied opinions and expectations for what an argument on recycling might contain.

THE TOPICS FOR COMMUNITY WRITING

As you select your topic for your informed opinion project, choose an issue about which you already have some knowledge and some opinion. You do not need to be an expert on the issue or an officially recognized member of the community for which you are writing; you can establish your credibility by appealing to the sense of community your ideal community of readers already has. By making an argument that considers the values and prior knowledge of the readers, you will establish yourself as someone with something to say to that community. To make sure that you appeal to readers' emotions, you might select a topic about which you already feel strongly. What is it that makes you angry, sad, or concerned? Is there some issue you feel strongly about and that people are generally discussing in any of the communities of which you are a member? What are the current issues at your school, in your community, in the nation, and in the world that cause you to feel that "something" needs to be done?

Do not simply select a topic and then repeat one of the usual arguments that you have heard. Choose a topic to which you can apply your own experiences and your original analysis. By avoiding the usual arguments, focusing on your own feelings and logic and experiences, and making a strong case for your own analysis and ideas, you might find that you come up with a contribution to the discussion.

THE PROBLEM APPROACH TO COMMUNITY WRITING

Informed opinions respond particularly well to the problem approach. Depending on your topic and who your ideal community of readers is, you could argue various elements of the problem approach to write your informed opinion.

- ❏ Is this a significant problem that deserves our attention? Believe it or not, many fine arguments about community issues are simply that we, as a community, are ignoring, missing, or not paying enough attention to something.

- ❏ How big a problem is it? By the same token, many arguments about community based issues revolve around the need to address a certain problem or issue. Considering that people and communities need to allocate resources based on what problems need the most attention, establishing that something is or is not worthy of attention may constitute a significant argument.

- ❏ How did it get to be a problem? Establishing just what causes a problem can be the first step to finding a solution. Even still, a significant argument can be made about how something got to be the way it is without suggesting a solution. As with every cause and effect argument, though, you must be sure to provide the causal chain. You can at least show the probability that one thing causes another.

- ❏ What will happen if we fail to address the problem? Establishing that a problem should be addressed before it becomes a bigger problem or before it leads to other problems can also be effective. Once again, this argument can be based on degrees of probability.

- ❏ What can be done about the problem? If you think that you might have a solution to the problem you are writing about, you might do well to remember that you do not always have to supply complete solutions to the problems. Often, you will do well to suggest even a partial solution to a problem.

Once again, the various elements of the problem approach build upon each other. If you are going to offer a solution to a problem, for instance, you might also have to demonstrate that the problem is big enough to warrant a solution or that your solution is addressing the appropriate cause.

THE TOULMIN METHOD AND COMMUNITY WRITING

The Toulmin method can work well for an informed opinion. For example, let us suppose that your claim (the purpose for your argument) is that your school should have a recycling program for aluminum cans. The grounds (the basic facts) might be that recycling aluminum cans is, in fact, good for the environment. The warrants for that claim (the major supporting points) might be the actual methods of the program and the reasons that the program would likely work—that students would participate, that the costs and inconvenience would not outweigh the benefits, etc. The backing for those warrants might include a survey of students to back up the first point and a cost analysis to back up the second. You might also need to include appropriate qualifiers and rebuttals to reassure students that the receptacles for cans would be kept clean or that the staff would actually have time for the resources or an acknowledgment that the program would not solve the problems of recycling altogether.

There are, of course, a myriad ways to apply the Toulmin method to any informed opinion. Still, this method will help you construct a logically sound argument that can be further supported by appeals to *ethos* and *pathos*.

POSSIBILITIES FOR NARRATIVE IN COMMUNITY WRITING

Narrative can strengthen your credibility (*ethos*) in an informed opinion. A narrative might show that you have personal experience with an issue, or it might show that you have knowledge about how the issue affects people. A narrative might also help you to generate an emotional response (*pathos*) in your reader if you include a story or stories about how real people have been affected by the issue. Or you might use a narrative as logical evidence (*logos*). Although we know that one or even a few stories about what happened to you or others will not generally supply enough logical evidence, a narrative can demonstrate that the issue does affect real people.

Writers sometimes discount the power of narrative structures to help make an argument. However, supplying narratives can help you make the issue more personal for both you and the reader. Narratives can supply credibility, an emotional appeal, and they can contribute to the logic of an argument.

In arguments about community issues, whether that community is a small or a large one, a personal narrative from the writer can demonstrate the real effects of something on an actual person. The narrative could also take the reader on the journey of realization that the writer took as he or she became aware of the issue or the steps the writer took to come to the project's conclusion. Narratives that relate the experiences of people who are affected by the issue are often included in these kinds of arguments to show that the present state of affairs actually does, can, or might cause people to suffer, which can contribute to the *pathos* and *logos* of the project. In this case, it might also be effective to ask the reader to imagine hypothetical narratives of what might or could happen. As with the editorial on Katrina, the author might have employed narratives about people who suffered the effects of Katrina's devastation or he might have included even more narratives about what could happen as a result of global warming.

POSSIBILITIES FOR ANALYSIS IN COMMUNITY WRITING

Supplying narrative structures or facts and statistics will not be enough to create an effective argument, of course. You will need to suggest what the narrative means and to interpret the facts and statistics so that your readers can understand what you think these things mean. Applying your own analysis to the situation will also help keep you from repeating the same arguments your readers have already heard. Even if you come to the same conclusions that others have, your analysis will give your writing a "fresh" quality to which readers might respond.

One effective strategy is to think about what objections your readers might have to your argument or to your analysis. You may wish to address those objections by including a section in which you address the possible objections, or you can anticipate and answer the objections to your arguments as they might arise in your readers' minds as they read your argument. Ignoring the obvious objections to your arguments can weaken it, but avoid presenting both sides of an argument and then suggesting that readers simply make up their own minds. Remember that outlining both sides of an issue and then merely suggesting that readers choose for themselves how to respond can be a waste of readers' time. Your job is generally to convince and persuade, not simply to invite readers to make up their own minds. As we have said, beginning writers sometimes feel the need to simply point out that one side says this and one side says that and that readers have to decide for themselves. This is especially true in this type of writing. What readers will want from you is your narratives, analysis, and arguments and not just an invitation to make up their own minds.

POSSIBILITIES FOR ARGUMENT IN COMMUNITY WRITING

As you are planning your informed opinion, consider your ideal community of readers and their expectations both for the genre and for the argument itself and consider where your writing might appear. If you are writing for a newspaper, newsletter, or blog, or a letter to an editor or a letter to an official, then read some similar writing to establish what readers of that genre might expect and how arguments in that genre are made. It is always tempting to rely on facts and statistics that you have found from other sources to make arguments, but what will matter most is that you apply your own argument skills to the issue. If you rely too much on what others have already argued, then you will most likely wind up repeating a familiar argument. What matters is that you construct your own argument, even if you come to the same conclusions as others. That is what will make your argument original. Narratives that describe your own experiences or those of people you know and analysis in which you apply your own thinking and ideas or make new connections are the support for your original argument. Keep in mind that the point of your project is that you want your readers to consider doing something or thinking something new after they read your project—that will be your purpose or your thesis. Then, design your analysis to support that purpose.

Reminding readers that you are part of the community or inviting readers to become part of the community can help. You will often see phrases such as "concerned and responsible citizens," "good, patriotic Americans," and "thinking adults" in arguments about community issues. The idea is to construct a relationship between you and your readers. Narratives can show your experience or the experiences of others, and new information from reliable sources will help your credibility, as will showing that you are aware of the objections that some might have to your evidence or argument. Appeals to emotion are vital, too, because they signal the importance of the issue. The logic of your argument will be most effective if your readers can "follow" your line of reasoning and understand how the support for your argument works.

AN INFORMED OPINION PROJECT

In this chapter, you learned that you are, in fact, a member of many different communities. For this project, you will produce an informed opinion that makes an argument addressing some specific issue or topic within one of those communities. It might help if you design your project as if it were to appear in some specific format such as a newspaper, a website, a magazine, or a "zine" that might be read by people who already have an interest in your topic. If you are producing a project that focuses on your school or your neighborhood, city, or state, then you might write an argument that could appear as an editorial or letter to the editor of your school or local newspaper.

Try to pick a topic about which you already have some information and some opinions, so that you do not have to conduct much research. You do not have to be an expert on the topic, but you should already possess some common knowledge on the subject and some strong opinions and ideas. Consider carefully whether you can address the topic in a way that avoids simply re-hashing arguments that readers are likely to have heard already. You will need to be able to add your ideas to one of the usual arguments, make new connections for the readers, or suggest a course of action for your readers. You might want to consider focusing your project by employing the problem approach or the Toulmin method to design your project. Remember that if you take the problem approach that you can argue that there is a problem or that the problem is a significant one. You might also argue that the problem is an effect of some specific cause or that the problem will lead to an undesired effect. You might choose to argue that some specific action needs to be taken to help alleviate the problem. Of course, some arguments will need to address more than one aspect of the problem approach to a topic.

Be sure to carefully think about who your ideal community of readers will be for the project: will you be writing for people who do not know much about the problem, who do not realize the problem is a significant one, who are probably inclined to agree with your perspective on the problem, or who are probably inclined to disagree with your perspective?

1. **Prewriting**: In this chapter, you were asked to think about yourself as a member of various communities. Think about how language is used within the community and how certain behaviors and attitudes are expected of the

members of that community before you write. Complete a short passage for your blog from one of the following ideas:

A. Write a short introduction to one of the communities to which you belong for someone who might just be joining that community. Imagine that you are welcoming someone into the community of world citizens, the citizens of America, the students at your school, the community of online gamers, the community of vegetarians, the people who follow a specific band or actor, or for those who enjoy a particular movie or store. Be sure to advise your readers of any specific behaviors that might be expected, special use of words, or social conventions that they will need to know about.

B. If you have selected a topic for your informed opinion project and know what you will be arguing, then try your hand at arguing the other side. Complete a short summary of the arguments that might be made against the argument you will be making in your informed opinion project.

C. Imagine that you have been given the opportunity to create a video blog that will be posted to your school's website about any issue that you think is important. In the blog, you will have the opportunity to say whatever you would like to say to everyone who visits the website of your school. You might offer a piece of advice for students considering whether to go to college or not, or you might ask viewers to take some action on an issue of importance or consider an idea—whatever you want to say to them. Do not waste the opportunity, though. Write out the five-minute blog as a script for yourself and, if you have access to a video camera, film the results.

2. **Drafting**: After you have come up with a possible topic for your informed opinion project, complete the Checklist of Questions for Establishing Exigency (p.44) and the Checklist of Questions for Structure (p.67). Check your classmates' blogs and consider what made their blog posts work well or what they might have done better so that you can apply those lessons to your project. Plot your argument carefully and remember to include appropriate appeals that might persuade your ideal community of readers. In addition to carefully considering the logic of your argument, you should also plan how you will establish your credibility and how you will construct an emotional appeal.

Narrative: Think about what kind of narrative structures you can apply in your informed opinion project and how those narratives can contribute to the *ethos*, *pathos*, and *logos* of your project. Will you tell about your own experiences with the topic or use a narrative about someone else's experiences?

Analysis: Remember that your job in this project is to provide some original thinking about the topic—to make new connections, to supply original analysis, or to suggest courses of action of which your readers might not be currently aware. Try not to simply repeat the arguments that you have already heard about the topic. Make sure and consider whether you will address major objections to your argument and how you will do so. Do not fall prey to the trap of merely outlining two different sides to an argument and then reminding the reader that they have to make up their own minds.

Argument: Remember to create *ethos* by reminding your readers that you are a member of the community or by asking them to become part of the community. Structure your argument carefully, as readers will expect that your logic will be sound. Try not to rely on too many sources as readers will be more interested in hearing your analysis of the facts and your thinking on the issue than they will be at just hearing you recite what others have said. Your logic, analysis, and careful consideration of the topic are what counts.

3. **Peer Review**: After you complete the first draft, send it out for peer review and complete the peer review questionnaires for your colleagues.

4. **The Visual**: Select an appropriate visual image to accompany your project. Complete the Checklist of Questions for Visuals (p. 204) and consider carefully how the visual will support your argument. Will you provide a chart or graph to help explain some statistics? Will you use an image that elicits an emotional response? Will you provide an icon or an image that illustrates something about the group and its membership?

5. **Revision and Proofing**: After you have selected your visual, completed your peer reviews, and received your peer-reviewed draft back, make revisions, and check your sentences. Check your work against the Checklist of Questions for Process (p.27). As always, you will want to read your final draft aloud before you consider it complete. After you are confident of your revision and proofing, save your file. Follow the instructions for uploading project two.

Peer Review Questionnaire
for the Informed Opinion Project

Your Name:

Title of the project you are peer reviewing:

Author of the project:

Answer the following questions about the project you are reviewing in a complete sentence or in a short paragraph.

1. Describe what "community" the ideal readers for this project would seem to belong to:

2. Summarize the writer's main argument in the project:

3. Describe what you like most about the project you are reviewing:

4. After reading the project, what question would you most like to ask the writer?

5. If you were to raise one objection to the writer's argument, what would that be?

6. Pick your favorite sentence from the project and copy it here. Then describe what you like about the sentence:

7. If the writer has included a visual image with the project, how do you think the visual adds to the project? Does it seem appropriate to the project? Does it contribute to the project? How? Could you suggest a more useful or appropriate visual for the project?

CHAPTER SIX

MAKING CHOICES ABOUT CULTURE AND THE MEDIA: WRITING A MEDIA CRITIQUE

> "Every time a message seems to grab us, and we think, 'I just might try it,' we are at the nexus of choice and persuasion that is advertising."
>
> --Andrew Hacker

THE SITUATION

Recently, the effect that "the media" has on our lives has become the subject of study in the fields of business, economics, psychology, education, communications, rhetoric, and the social sciences. In fact, private and public institutes now study the influence of the media on us and examine how the media reflects and affects our American and global cultures. Some researchers wonder whether we are exposed to too much materialism, sex, violence, bad language, and negative stereotyping in the media, and there are charges that the media is corrupting the information we get about the world. The sheer volume of research on the effects that the media has on our lives indicates that the issue is of grave importance to many people.

Technically, the word "media" refers not just to radio, television, film, music, and the Internet. The word also applies to print media such as newspapers, books, magazines, and even "outdoor" media such as signs and billboards. Wherever you find the media, you will also find advertising, of course. In fact, it is interesting how much space is taken up in the media by communication whose primary goal is to sell us something. In larger cities, advertisement has spilled out of the traditional categories and taken over almost every available space. The walls of buildings are turned into advertisements; buses are plastered with ads, and people watch ads on video screens as they ride in elevators or taxi cabs. Even if you live in a small town, you are exposed to hundreds of advertisements every day. Pop-ups appear on your computer screen, search engines such as Yahoo and Google feature sponsored links and banner ads, and for each hour that you watch television, at least ten or 12 minutes is spent viewing ads (often more). To expand these opportunities, marketers have now begun to embed advertisement into our phones and other devices. Many of the applications, or "aps" for cellphones and hand-held computers are thinly-veiled advertisements. For example, one of the new iPhone applications offers to find the closest Starbucks for you.

Advertisers are also learning that if they disguise their ads, they might have a better chance at getting past the "screens" that we all throw up around ourselves to filter out the onslaught of advertising. Companies pay to have characters in movies or on television shows use their products. If a character drinks a certain soft drink or drives a particular brand of car, then the company has probably paid to have their product featured as part of the content of that movie or show. Some companies—most notably the makers of computer games, sports equipment, clothing, automobiles, and computer equipment—actually pay regular people to use or wear or drive their products where crowds of potential buyers gather. The latest and "hottest" cars are sometimes parked at college campus events so that potential buyers can see them. Can you be sure that the "regular guy" who showed you his new computer game this morning at the coffee shop was not paid by the company to do so?

Considering how awash we are in media, it is no wonder that some people are concerned with how much advertisement we see and with political and cultural bias in the media. Others are concerned that the violence, sexual content, and racial and sexual stereotypes that we see may have a negative influence. Do these people have a reason to be concerned? Unless we are children, we make up our own minds about what we buy and what we believe, right? Aren't we able to separate the fiction from the reality, the real news from the sensationalistic reporting and bias, and the ads from the entertainment?

To a large extent, we are, of course. Still, making good choices within the flood of media information takes awareness of how media texts work. Fortunately, that awareness can be developed. In order to make good choices about what news to consider valid, what entertainment is appropriate, and what product to buy, it helps if you learn to examine media texts more carefully to establish how the "authors" design their content to persuade you that certain news is appropriate, that certain content is entertaining, and that a particular brand or product is "right" for you.

You can take comfort in the fact that you have no doubt already developed this media awareness to a large degree. Children can have problems separating the ads from the programming (which is why laws regulate children's entertainment and advertising), but most adults have developed skills that allow them to discriminate between advertisement and content and to separate the valid claims from the fraudulent. Still, learning to respond (or not to respond) to advertising in order to make good choices is only one set of skills you need to be "media-savvy." After all, it is not just advertisement that seeks to persuade. News programs, newspapers, and magazines are, in effect, arguing that the items they report are the relevant ones, and, regardless of their attempts to be objective and fair, each news outlet cannot help but put the stamp of its own perspective on the news. Television, movie, and music producers are also making a sort of argument for their perspective. Stand-up comics, television sit-coms and dramas, action movies, love stories, and popular singers and songwriters are all, in a way, arguing that their particular views of the world are entertaining, valid, and worth "buying." Since all media is a form of argument, it helps you make good choices if you can examine how rhetoric works in the media to promote ideas and values.

At first, thinking about the media in this way might seem like a classic case of "over-analyzing" things. Take, for instance, advertising. After all, how complex can it be to design a successful ad? You want people to buy the product, so you tell them what it does and how well it does it so that they can compare your brand with other brands and decide if they want to buy. But it is not that simple, is it? In fact, it does not take too much analysis to realize that there is much more at work in most ads than just a simple argument to buy the product.

Imagine that you are designing an advertisement. Would you be happy that only people who legitimately need your product buy it? What if you could encourage people to believe that they need your product even if they do not? After all, did you know that you needed a cell phone that told you where the nearest coffee shop was before you saw one? How do people know that they "need" a shirt with an Abercrombie and Fitch logo? You might be tempted to answer that you buy these things because they are convenient, because you simply want them, and because they make your life better. Chances are that you have been influenced by the rhetoric of advertising, though, whether you are aware of it or not.

Advertisers are not just in the business of promoting their product based on its usefulness. They are also in the business of creating desire for their products, and to do that they use rhetoric. Just as you consider what values you might appeal to in order to persuade your ideal community of readers, so, too, do advertisers and the "authors" of televisions shows, movies, new broadcasts, songs, billboards, and newspaper articles consider their rhetorical appeals, their ideal community of readers (the "target audience"), and the values that audience might share.

One thing to remember is that the media is motivated primarily by business concerns. Even news and entertainment outlets are funded by advertisement. There are, of course, also laws that dictate fairness, appropriateness, and validity in the media to help protect the public. By law, advertisers cannot make false or misleading claims. Movie, television, and music producers must warn viewers when their products contain "adult" content. Television and radio networks are required to give equal opportunities for political candidates to buy time. Most people who work in or own various media "outlets" are aware that violating the public trust can seriously damage their credibility. However, the primary motivation behind what you see and hear in the media is advertising revenue.

This is not to imply that people who work in the media are manipulating us into believing that reality shows are "real," that the news is complete and free of bias, or that the products they advertise are really best for us. The media uses certain rhetorical appeals and follows trends because that rhetoric and those trends help sell products. In a way, news outlets report the news that viewers and readers want to know about. Editors generally design magazines and newspapers to appeal to a specific target audience, and advertisers are interested in finding out what consumers will buy. It is easy to criticize the media for forcing certain trends on the public, but if a movie is bad, if a news report is irrelevant or false, or if a product is useless, then no amount of clever rhetoric will persuade very many people to tune in or to buy. People who work in the media identify and reinforce certain trends, but the messages would not be effective if they were not giving the public what it wants. Most people who work in the media realize that consumers make choices about what they watch, read, and buy, and so they design their content to use the same basic appeals that we have learned to get the desired response. Our responsibility, as media-savvy readers, is to focus our rhetorical skills on "reading" the media carefully. After all, blaming the media for our lack of judgment, depth, and sophistication is irresponsible. Still, it helps to remember that behind every movie, television show, song, news report, editorial, article and ad are people whose job it is to persuade us to enjoy this particular message and to buy the product.

This does not mean that it is wrong to simply enjoy a movie or a new song because it is exciting or provocative, and it does not mean that you have to over-analyze every interesting advertisement that you see. However, learning to "read" the media will help you become a smarter consumer, and becoming media-savvy requires that you think about each movie, television show, song, news report, article, and advertisement as a form of "text" that employs rhetoric. These "texts" are more complex than simple words on a page, too. They also employ color, action, and images to persuade. However, you are already familiar with how images can contribute to rhetorical appeals, and to become more media-savvy you can also rely on your ability to recognize narrative, analysis, and argumentative structures and on your ability to understand how appeals to *ethos*, *pathos*, and *logos* are constructed.

One important aspect of the media is the use of **cultural myths** to help make the argument. For instance, one of the most famous images in advertising is the Marlboro cowboy. Why would it be advantageous for a cigarette company to use the image of a cowboy to sell cigarettes? The answer is that the cowboy is a cultural myth. In this case, the word "myth" does not designate something that is not true; instead, it stands for the idea that complex meanings have become attached to certain symbols, characters, settings, or narratives. Over time, the cowboy has come to symbolize the ideas of rugged individuality, self-reliance, toughness, and masculinity. As such, artists, producers, and advertisers have made use of the cultural myth of the American cowboy because people connect that image with those values. You want to be a macho, self-sufficient, rugged individual? Smoke Marlboro cigarettes. In fact, the Marlboro Man was such a successful advertising campaign that this particular set of images have become cultural icons (http://adage.com/century/icon01.html).

Cultural myths can also be recognized in movies, news reports, and popular song. How many movies have you seen where the "hero" is an individual who operates outside the system, takes the law into his own hands, and foils the bad guy with determination, guts, cunning, and action? We see this hero so much that we do not question the link between heroism and individual action, bravery, and initiative. That is because this particular character and this narrative evoke a cultural myth that we have been conditioned to respond to favorably. How many movies have you seen in which the female character has to "save" her male love interest by getting him to see that he has to change, or where she, herself, must be saved (often literally) by the hero before she can win his love? These characters and narratives are linked to popular cultural myths that we have been taught to "read" and respond to in a specific way. We feel good when the action hero saves the fair maiden, even if we know that we are primarily responding to emotions and logic that have been reinforced by years and years of cultural representation.

The relationship between these cultural myths and the values they support is complex. Does the media's use of these cultural myths reinforce belief in specific ideas of heroism or feminity, or do these myths simply reflect the values that people already have? The answer is that cultural myths both reflect popular values and reinforce them. The mistake would be to assume either that the media cynically manipulates consumers by creating and promoting these cultural myths or that these cultural myths represent the "natural" way of the world. The relationship between cultural myths and human psychology are complex. Men are not always strong and in-charge and women are not always helpless and in need of being rescued. While we may question these stereotypes, they still make us feel comfortable at some level.

Even news reports make use of cultural myths. We have been conditioned to respond emotionally to the story of the beautiful actress or musical "diva" who cannot control her temper and who flits from relationship to relationship; we watch in morbid fascination as musicians and actors fall prey to drink and drugs. News report are, perhaps, full of these stories because, in some way, we need them to feel better about ourselves.

As you sharpen your ability to "read" media texts, remember that colors and images also work to strengthen rhetorical appeals. Ads for menthol cigarettes often contain blues and greens because we associate those colors with coolness. Studies performed by major universities have shown that our brains respond to colors in certain, predictable ways (http://www.colormatters.com/brain.html). The man who uses a certain body spray is encouraged to imagine himself in the mildly erotic situations featured in the ads. Ads for expensive vodka feature sophisticated art to encourage readers to link the consumption of the product with a sophisticated image.

Once you begin to read media texts in this way, you may actually become more interested in how various images and cultural myths work in those texts, and learning to read media texts more carefully—more skeptically—has practical benefits. You will never become totally immune to the influence of media persuasion, but you may become a more savvy media consumer. You will certainly become more keenly aware of the uses of rhetoric in the world around you.

THE GENRE—THE MEDIA CRITIQUE

Generally, writing about the media takes the form of a **media critique**. The use of the word "critique," however, is not meant to imply that only negative things must be said. The objective is not to "bash" the media but to analyze how the text is constructed, how it appeals to its ideal community of readers, and how it employs rhetoric, images, and cultural myths to make its arguments. In other words, the idea is to examine a particular media text to discover how it works—to uncover how the images and the text appeal to the target audience through the promotion of values associated with the rhetoric and cultural myths the text employs. The text might be a television show, a movie, a song, a news report, a newsworthy event, or an advertisement. Often, a particular ad or movie or news report might be compared to other similar texts to help make the critique, or the critique might take as its subject an entire "type" of media text. For instance, the critique might examine the idea of the "action movie" or the "radio talk show," or analyze a specific "outlet" of the media, such as The Food Channel, the Fox News Network, or Disney. The author of the critique might discuss the entire range of advertisements for various SUVs or fashion advertisement in general to reveal how rhetoric and cultural myths are used in this form of media text. The purpose of the media critique is to analyze the text, to establish who the ideal community of readers for the text is, and to determine how cultural myths are employed to help the text make its argument.

As we have noted, the obvious message of any advertisement is to "buy the product." Similarly, the message of any movie, television show, or popular song is, on one level, simply to be entertained by it. In the news media, the message is, at first glance, simply that this news item is important and newsworthy. However, the goal of the critique is to look beyond these simple goals and to analyze how the text employs the appeals of rhetoric and how it links itself to popular cultural myths. Your job as media critic is to uncover and reveal those appeals and myths in order to make an argument about how the particular text works.

In a way, you are making an argument about what the themes of the media text are. These themes are similar to the themes we find in literature. In fact, media critiques often use familiar terms from literary analysis such as "character," "setting," "symbol," "plot," and "theme." You may wish to fall back on these terms in your description of the media text; however, as with analysis of literary texts, you should limit your summary of the text and concentrate on the analysis.

Let us examine two critiques to establish how the genre can work. The first is from noted media critic Rob Walker, who writes for the online journal, *Slate*:

> A *man, whose face we never see, is folding laundry in his bright and airy loft. Specifically he's folding a pair of women's underwear, white with little yellow flowers. Inoffensive music plays in the background as a man's voice narrates. (This is a well-known actor who, as part of the campaign's gimmick, isn't named; I'll say who it is below.) "When we first got married, she'd wear really sexy underwear, like you see in underwear ads," the young husband muses. Here we see his blond wife, I guess in a flashback, cavorting sexily in black undergarments in the dark. A quick montage finds her looking not a day older, but in the morning light and a roomy pajama top. "After a while," the narrator continues, "she started wearing the kind of underwear that I saw in the hamper when I was a kid." Here one of the shots is of him sort of handling the underwear. "There's something oddly reassuring about thin, washed-out, cotton underwear, with little yellow flowers." Some Diet Coke cans are in evidence as the laundry-and-domesticity montage winds down and closes on an image of the blond wife and the "That Certain Something" tag line.*

This is a strange ad. It's a really strange ad. For starters, let's just pause to note that Diet Coke apparently wants its brand to be as familiar to you as old underwear. OK? Now, let's put that aside. What's this bit about his wife's underwear being like "the kind of underwear that I saw in the hamper when I was a kid"? What does that mean? It's like his mother's underwear? Who among you entertains a wistful nostalgia for your mother's underwear? Let's see a show of hands, please. Actually, let's not.

The narrator then goes on to say that there is something "oddly reassuring about thin, washed-out cotton underwear." Well, if he finds that reassuring, I will agree with the "oddly" part. So, let's clarify what that "certain something" about Diet Coke is. Diet Coke is as "reassuring" as "thin, washed-out" underwear, reminiscent of your mother's, but worn by your wife? Run that by your shrink sometime.

Perhaps I'm being too literal? OK, then, forget the underwear, what's the basic theme of this little story? We have a young married couple. She used to wear sexy underwear. Although they're clearly still young, this couple has gotten over that sort of thing and settled into a less exciting, quotidian groove, in which they will presumably remain until parted by death. And the husband finds this reassuring. I have nothing against the idea of domestic bliss, but usually the sort of epiphany that this man is having (i.e., we have reached the end of a certain road here and can only hope for comfort, never again excitement) is an occasion for deep existential, how-did-I-get-here angst. But the brand managers of Diet Coke have a different take--it is as if they have chosen to say, "Here you go, pal; enjoy an ice-cold, refreshing can of your very mortality." Maybe that's the certain something: a resigned sense of fatalism.

Anyway, the narrator is Ben Affleck, who delivers his peculiar lines with absolute conviction-which proves, I suspect, that he does have some acting ability after all.

Notice that Walker begins with a description of the ad, blending a summary of the images, the action, and the narration. He describes the music that accompanies the ad and the words of the voice-over narrator, who speaks from the husband's point of view as he folds clothes. Walker suggests that the authors of this ad are attempting to connect certain cultural myths to the product. He argues that cultural myths about the typical American household are employed to appeal to the values of the typical

American consumer, and suggests that the target audience is somewhat older and more settled. The husband seems "oddly" content that she has given up lingerie for underwear that reminds him of his mother. This seems a bit strange, as Walker points out. However, Walker makes the connection between this cultural myth—that it is ok for life to "settle into a less exciting, quotidian groove" (did you look up the word "quotidian?")—and the product: Diet Coke. In effect, the cultural myth suggests a value: that after marriage one settles down and becomes content with comfortable things. This is a value that the target audience probably shares. So what does Diet Coke have to gain from linking itself to such values?

Let us examine another critique, this time from editorialist Jim Rutenberg:

> *Osama bin Laden, according to Fox News Channel anchors, analysts and correspondents, is "a dirtbag," "a monster" overseeing a "web of hate." His followers in AI Qaeda are "terror goons." Taliban fighters are "diabolical" and "henchmen."*

> *Ever since the terrorist attacks on Sept. 11, the network has become a sort of headquarters for viewers who want their news served up with extra patriotic fervor. In the process, Fox has pushed television news where it has never gone before: to unabashed and vehement support of a war effort, carried in tough-guy declarations often expressing thirst for revenge.*

> *The network, owned by the News Corporation of Rupert Murdoch, has always had a reputation--one it disavows--of being politically conservative. But its demeanor since Sept. 11 has surprised even its critics. The network is encouraging correspondents and writers to tap into their anger and let it play out in a way that reminds some rivals and press critics of the war drumbeat of the old Hearst papers and the ideologically driven British tabloids.*

> *The usual anchor role of delivering the news free of personal opinion has been altered to include occasional asides. On a recent edition of the network's 5 p.m. program, "The Big Story," the anchor, John Gibson, said that military tribunals were needed to send the following message to terrorists: "There won't be any dream team for you. There won't be any Mr. Johnnie hand-picking jurors and insisting that the headgear don't fit, you must acquit. Uh-uh. Not this time, pal."*

> *Geraldo Rivera, now a Fox war correspondent in Afghanistan, has said that he would consider killing Osama bin Laden himself if he*

came across him. (In a live transmission from Taliqan on Thursday, he acknowledged carrying a gun for self defense.) So far, the journalistic legacy of this war would seem to be a debate over what role journalism should play at a time of war. The Fox News Channel is the incarnation of a school of thought that the morally neutral practice of journalism is now inappropriate.

This critique comes in the form of a traditional argument, complete with a purpose-statement and examples that serve as support. After an introduction that provides a context for the argument, Rutenberg asserts his thesis: that Fox news has changed the course of news reporting by pushing it "where it has never gone before" to support the war in Iraq. Such an accusation requires evidence, and Rutenberg cites two examples: the "aside" of the news anchor and the narrative about Geraldo Rivera. For Rutenberg, this change is obviously bad, which is evidenced in his choice of words like "unabashed." This critique is obviously directed toward a readership that might be inclined to believe that news reports should be unbiased or should at least appear to be unbiased.

A ▶ *Activity:*

Form small groups and examine the two media critiques above to see if you can further uncover how their rhetoric works. See if you can answer the following questions without getting too caught up in whether you agree or disagree with the major arguments in each critique. How do the authors establish their *ethos*? Are they successful? Can you further describe the ideal community of readers for each critique? What values might these readers have and how do the authors appeal to those values? What emotions are elicited by these critiques? Can you find any other cultural myths at work in these critiques?

The Ideal Community of Readers for the Media Critique

When you are thinking about the ideal community of readers for your media critique, remember that the idea that media texts reflect and promote certain values might be a somewhat new one for some readers. Still, the media critic assumes that readers will already be fairly skilled at understanding media messages, although the terminology might be new to them, as it probably was to you.

Since advertisers know that people view a wide variety of media texts each day, they also realize that to make their ads "stand out" they need to employ interesting appeals. As such, you will often find that advertisements are some of the most innovative media texts you can find (not all of them, of course). Sometimes, the ads will actually try to appeal to viewers by making fun of themselves, by purposefully calling attention to the fact that they are using various appeals and making reference to cultural myths, or by somehow "twisting" those cultural myths. In short, ads often contain some of the most interesting and self-aware rhetoric.

Since the relationship between cultural myth and human psychology is quite complex, media critics must be careful to draw the evidence for their arguments about media texts from the texts themselves. The readers of media critiques will likely expect sophisticated analysis supported by evidence taken directly from the text.

Since everyone views advertisements daily, you might think that the ideal community of readers for media critique is quite large. Still, you can focus on writing for an ideal community of readers who might be interested in your critique because of the type of product that is advertised, or you can focus on writing for readers who are interested in how a particular type of cultural myth is employed by the ad. Will your readers be interested in your analysis of an automobile ad primarily because they are interested in automobiles or will they be interested because the ad employs cultural myths about freedom and "maleness?"

The Topics for the Media Critique

One way to begin to pick a topic for your media critique is to look through some ads and see what you, yourself, are interested in. Are you interested in the ad primarily because it promotes a product or a type of product that interests you, or are you primarily interested in the ad because of the way it employs certain kinds of cultural myth or myths? In other words, are you interested in the ad for eye makeup because you buy and use lots of makeup or are you interested in the ad because of the way that it employs cultural myths about women and beauty? That will help you pick your ideal community of readers and it will help you focus your critique. The purpose of your critique, then, will be to inform your readers about the ad and then to argue that this ad promotes its product by employing specific cultural myths and rhetorical appeals.

You will not have to spend lots of time reminding your readers that the goal of the ad is to sell them something. Your readers will want your analysis of *how* the text works to sell its product and, in particular, how the text uses or reinforces cultural myths to make its argument. Do not expend too many words describing the ad, except for giving the reader a quick summary. Focus whatever description you include on the parts that support your thesis. One possible way to focus your writing is to plan your critique to answer one of the following questions:

❑ How does this ad use a particular cultural myth to make its appeals?

❑ How does this ad reinforce popular belief in a cultural myth?

❑ How does this ad provide a particular twist to a popular cultural myth?

You could also use the problem approach to help you find a topic and plan a structure for your media critique.

THE PROBLEM APPROACH TO THE MEDIA CRITIQUE

Although the main focus of the media critique is analysis, we know that even analysis presents a form of argument. In fact, using the problem approach can help you focus your analysis of the advertisement in a way that is more interesting for readers.

❑ Is this a significant problem that deserves our attention? The job of any writing project is, first, to persuade readers that the topic deserves their attention. Focusing on this question will provide the reader with some reason to care how specific cultural myths are employed to sell a product or a type of product. For instance, does the way women are generally portrayed in advertisement matter? Why? Is the issue important enough to deserve our attention?

❑ How big a problem is it? Perhaps your readers are unaware just how much these cultural myths influence people. In fact, people often think that these cultural myths are innocent and that those who fall prey to the rhetoric of advertisement are somehow deserving of it. You could choose to argue that the use of specific cultural myths to sell a particular product or type of product does have negative consequences.

❑ How did it get to be a problem? Here, you might discuss how you think the cultural myths you are writing about came to have the power to influence us. Why do we respond to these myths? What is the history of these myths?

❑ What will happen if we fail to address the problem? You might want to write about what will happen if we do not become more aware of how media rhetoric works or what will happen if we protect those who are too young to make informed choices from media rhetoric. Are there cultural myths at work in advertisement that have consequences for people beyond just the fact that they may wind up buying the product? What else are they "buying" when they respond to these cultural myths?

❏ What can be done about the problem? You might also suggest how people might become aware or more educated about these cultural myths and the way they are used in the media. You could discuss whether you think certain types of ads (children's ads for instance) should be regulated.

As you can see, focusing on the problem approach to help you plan for your media critique will encourage you to plan your essay so that you present an actual argument based on your analysis.

THE TOULMIN METHOD AND THE MEDIA CRITIQUE

Once again, although the media critique is a form of analysis, it is also argument. As such, the Toulmin method can be used to develop a topic and a plan for the structure of your media critique.

Let us imagine that the claim of your media critique (the purpose for your argument) is that new car ads use cultural myths about American independence and world power to sell larger automobiles and trucks. The grounds (the basic facts) for that claim might be that Americans do, in fact, buy and drive larger cars and trucks than people in other countries. The warrants for that claim (the major supporting points) would be your analysis of those cultural myths and how they are used in automobile ads, and perhaps why they work or the history of those myths. The backing might then be your close analysis of the ads and their specific deployment of these myths. In the media critique, qualifiers and rebuttals are particularly important because this type of analysis produces generalities that some people might see as stereotypes or as ideas that do not apply to them (not everyone drives a large car or truck). One of the common reactions to media analysis is that people will think they are somehow immune to these cultural myths or that your analysis is weak because it includes stereotypes that do not apply to everyone. The media critique is, by its nature, an analysis that takes specific things—in this case cultural myths, specific types of ads, and certain demographics—and makes generalizations about them. As such, you will want to signal to your readers that you know you might be making some generalizations.

POSSIBILITIES FOR NARRATIVE IN THE MEDIA CRITIQUE

Often, media critiques will have strong authorial "voice." In the two critiques above, you will find that both authors' personalities are evident. Walker is humorous and sarcastic; Rutenberg is forceful and vigorous. At first glance, you might be tempted to say that these critiques are merely the opinions of these interesting authors. Remember, though, that opinions are arguable as long as there are some values in question.

Readers will understand that every analysis is the product of the specific critic's analysis and does not represent some kind of "truth" about what the media text means. In fact, that is why *ethos* is so important in media critiques, and critiques often contain narrative, or at least a strong tone, that allows the reader to get a sense of who the critic is and what he or she values. Sometimes, the critic will describe his or her encounter with the ad as a way to provide some narrative structure and to strengthen the appeal to *ethos*. In this project, do not be afraid to be personal, to offer your opinion, and to reveal your personal reactions. Just remember to reinforce your credibility by supporting your analysis with evidence from the media text itself.

POSSIBILITIES FOR ANALYSIS IN THE MEDIA CRITIQUE

Your job in this project is to identify the use of one or more cultural myths, to explain how the text uses or twists those myths, and to supply analysis of how various parts of the text—the characters, plot and narrative, the colors and images, and the words—provide evidence for your analysis.

You can begin with a summary of the ad or by describing your encounter with the ad, but move quickly to a statement about how the ad works (your thesis) and then to your analysis. Does your analysis of the colors and the images in the text support your claim? Can you find evidence to suggest that the target audience for that advertisement will be persuaded by those values?

Often, the placement of the ad will be important to identifying the target audience. During the daytime, more television ads are targeted to women viewers or feature household products, since the advertisers and producers make the assumption that more women are home and watching television or that whoever is home is engaged in washing clothes, cooking, or cleaning. Advertisers run more beer and car ads during football games, as they assume that more men are watching. Magazines are specifically targeted to various audiences, and you will find their advertisements are geared toward that **demographic**. Despite the fact that this is obvious stereotyping, advertisers make these assumptions as they plan their ads and when they schedule them. In addition, advertisers design their ads to appeal to values that they assume this target audience will recognize and embrace. Thus, the placement of the ad can also give you a sense of the target audience and help you uncover what cultural myths are being employed.

POSSIBILITIES FOR ARGUMENT IN THE MEDIA CRITIQUE

Your argument will be that the ad employs or twists certain cultural myths to appeal to specific values to which the target audience might respond. You might need to make some generalizations about the target audience, about the cultural myths being employed, and about the values the ad uses to make its appeals. Not all women stay at home during the day, and men also do the laundry, the cooking, and the housecleaning. Not all men watch football, drink beer, and worry about their cars. However, advertisers often use these generalizations to target their ads. No advertiser can take into account all the various viewers who might see the ad, so they take a "bottom line" approach to targeting an audience. These assumptions will often point the way to the successful analysis. Still, it will not be enough to point out that the generalizations made by the ad are inadequate when applied to every person. In other words, it is not enough to say "I do not respond to that advertisement because I do not fit that stereotype" as the thesis of your media critique. Ads employ various appeals because they generally work. Often, when you see an ad that employs obvious stereotyping or blatant appeals, it also contains a twist on that appeal that encourages the target audience to respond to the ad in spite of the stereotyping.

Focus your critique on identifying at least one cultural myth in the ad. Discuss how that myths appeals to the values of the target audience, and supply evidence drawn from various parts of the ad to argue that they contribute to the appeals.

A MEDIA CRITIQUE PROJECT

In this chapter, you learned that media texts use cultural myths to appeal to the values of their target audience. For this project, you will produce a media critique that analyzes how a specific magazine advertisement uses cultural myths to make its appeals to the target audience for the ad. You may choose to write about an advertisement that appears in any type of magazine, and you should take into account the type of magazine in which the advertisement appears and how that helps to define the target audience. As an alternative, you could choose to examine a television or radio advertisement, but if you do, you will need to have some way to save or copy the ad so that you can view it as many times as you need to, or you might be able to find a video of the ad on Youtube or on the company's website. As an alternative, you might pick an ad that is repeated frequently and take very good notes when you see it.

Your critique will be base on your analysis of how the advertisement uses cultural myths to make its appeals. Consider carefully whether the advertisement you are analyzing makes assumptions about its target audience and then uses those assumptions to appeal to certain values. Remember that the quality of your evidence and your analysis is key to writing a successful media critique, as that is what will support your claims about how the advertisement works. Do not spend too much time summarizing the advertisement but focus instead on your analysis of the text and what cultural myths it employs to make its appeals. Your job is to make the connections between the text, its target audience, its use of cultural myths, and its appeals.

You can assume that your ideal community of readers has some experience with reading media texts, so be sure to concentrate on your particular analysis and the evidence that supports that analysis and not on making the argument that the advertisement is trying to sell something. Your readers will know that.

1. **Prewriting**: In this chapter, you were asked to think about how cultural myths are employed by the media and how those cultural myths appeal to certain values the target audience might share. Complete a short passage for your blog from one of the following ideas:

   A. Imagine that you are an advertising writer who has been employed to write a new advertisement for a particular product of your choosing. Try to identify the target audience for the product and what values that target audience might share. Write a short summary of a television ad for this product that targets that specific audience, makes use of some appropriate cultural myths, and appeals to values that that audience might share. You might actually film the ad if you have access to a camera. If you are able to "film" your ad, be sure to pay attention to color and tone and character in setting the scene and in "casting" characters for your ad. You might post this ad as a video blog.

B. Watch a few half-hour news programs and see if you can identify a particular story that you see repeated. Take notes on how the specific elements of the story are used and how they are treated differently from newscast to newscast. Then write your own short news report on the story, emphasizing the repeated elements and providing your own "twist" to the story. If you can, you could record these news stories and present a "montage" of the coverage as a video blog.

C. Watch a television show and write down or record the advertisements that are aired during the show. Create a short summary of what types of ads are featured and what this reveals about who the target audience might be for the show and what values this target audience might share.

2. **Drafting**: Before you begin to draft your media critique, complete the Checklist of Questions for Establishing Exigency (p.44) and the Checklist of Questions for Structure (p.67). Check your classmates' blogs and consider what made their blog posts work well or what they might have done better so that you can apply those lessons to your project. Carefully decide what your main claim is before you write. Remember to focus on what cultural myth or myths the advertisement employs and how that helps the advertisement make its appeals to the target audience.

Narrative: Remember that a part of your credibility in the media critique might be linked to the narrative structure and the tone of your critique. You might use a narrative to introduce the ad—often, media critiques will recount the writer's experiences as he or she comes across the ad. The idea is to let the reader into your mind as you analyze the advertisement. Your credibility will depend on your careful analysis, of course, but you might also think about bringing a bit of your personality to the critique to reinforce the emotions you want your readers to experience as they read your critique and to help establish your credibility. This narrative might also help the logical appeal. Remember that your analysis is based on your personal and informed opinion about how the ad works; as such, your credibility as a media critic is paramount.

Analysis: Careful analysis of the advertisement is key to this project, as the claims you make about how the advertisement uses cultural myths to appeal to the values of the target audience should be linked to evidence that you draw directly from the advertisement. Make a claim about how the advertisement works, about what cultural myths it employs, about what values it appeals to, and then support those claims with evidence. As you analyze the various parts of the advertisement, focus on how they relate to the cultural myths the ad employs. Remember that your job in this project is to provide some original analysis about the ad--to make new connections between the parts of the ad, the cultural myths they allude to, the values those cultural myths support, and the target audience for the ad. Try not fall into the trap of simply reporting that the advertisement is trying to sell something. Focus instead on how the ad uses cultural myths to sell the product or service to a specific target audience.

Argument: Your argument will be that the advertisement makes use of specific cultural myths to appeal to the values that the target audience for the ad might share. Structure your argument carefully to include as many parts of the advertisement as you can and focus on how all these parts support your analysis. Basically, you might construct the argument as a claim supported by examples. The examples will be the parts of the advertisement that you describe, analyze, and relate back to your claim. Your logic, analysis, and careful consideration of the topic are what counts.

3. **Peer Review**: After you complete the first draft, complete the peer review process.

4. **The Visual**: Select an appropriate visual image to accompany your project. You might go the website for the product and download a video of the ad or a picture of the product or the logo for the company. Many ads (and parodies of ads) are available on sites like Youtube, but be sure to supply a credit for this and all visuals you download from other sites. Complete the Checklist of Questions for Visuals (p. 204) and consider carefully how the visual will support your argument.

5. **Revision and Proofing**: After you have selected your visual, completed your peer reviews, and received your peer-reviewed draft back, make revisions and check your sentences. Check your work against the Checklist of Questions for Process (p. 27). As always, you will want to read your final draft aloud before you consider it complete. After you are confident of your revision and proofing, save your file. Follow the instructions for uploading the project.

Peer Review Questionnaire for the Media Critique

Your Name:

Title of the project you are peer reviewing:

Author of the project:

Answer the following questions about the project you are reviewing in a complete sentence or in a short paragraph.

1. Summarize the primary cultural myth that the writer claims the advertisement uses:

2. What is your reaction to the advertisement? Have you seen it before? Do you agree with the writer's analysis of the advertisement?

3. Do you think the writer provides enough analysis of the advertisement or is too much space taken up with description of the ad?

4. What is the "tone" of the project? Sarcastic? Academic? Humorous? Serious? How appropriate is that tone to the project?

5. Is there anything that you would suggest that the writer add to the critique?

6. What do you think of the title of the critique? Is it appropriate and interesting? If not, could you suggest another title?

7. Pick your favorite sentence from the project and copy it here. Then describe what you like about the sentence:

8. If the writer has included a visual image with the project, how do you think the visual adds to the project? Does it seem appropriate to the project? Does it contribute to the project? How? Could you suggest a more useful or appropriate visual for the project?

CHAPTER SEVEN

MAKING VOCATIONAL CHOICES: WRITING A VOCATIONAL INFORMATIVE PROJECT

> "We must hold a man amenable to reason for the choice of his daily craft or profession. It is not an excuse any longer for his deeds that they are the custom of his trade. What business has he with an evil trade?"
>
> --Ralph Waldo Emerson

THE SITUATION

There is an old saying that if you "do what you love, then the money will follow." This suggests that you should follow your heart and choose a career that expresses what you most want out of life, and there is probably some wisdom in this advice. After all, would you really be willing to work at a job you hate for the rest of your life even if it paid well, or would you be willing to forego some monetary reward in order to feel that the work you do is satisfying and rewarding in other ways? Perhaps the advice to choose your career based on what you really want to do rather than what you think will make you the most money comes from a time when economic futures were more easily predicted; however, the world is full of people who wish they had followed their hearts instead of the money.

Without a doubt, the prospects of the typical college student of today are a bit more uncertain than they were for those who went to college only a few years ago. In order to keep up with the globalization of the economy, the rapid advance of technology, and the changing demands of doing business, new types of professionals are needed every year, and those professionals must be able to adapt to change more quickly. When you consider how quickly things change, it is not at all surprising that many people now work in jobs that are not obviously related to their major in college. The chances of successfully predicting which professions will be most in demand or most lucrative five or ten years from now is increasingly difficult. That said, choosing to enter any profession simply because you believe that it will lead to successful employment or monetary reward can be a risky proposition. Simply put, what's "hot" on the job market today may not be hot in four years.

There was a time when most students chose a profession either before they got to college or while they were in college, and then they followed that path throughout their entire academic and professional careers. That idea still seems very attractive, and there are persons who dream of becoming a doctor or a lawyer or a teacher or a journalist, go to college to study in that discipline, and then work their entire lives in that vocation. Today, however, there is less likelihood of that scenario. The Bureau of Labor Statistics (http://www.bls.gov/), which is an excellent resource for researching occupations and professions, now estimates that the average person will change careers three times over his or her working life.

Obviously, there are college students who are committed to specific courses of study and professions because of their long-term personal goals. Some of these students have felt a calling for a vocation for a long time, and some are students who have already been in the job force and are now training for some specific career change or for advancement. Still, a great many students are ambivalent about career goals, especially in their first few years of college. If that is the case for you, then you should take some of the pressure off and allow yourself some time to explore alternatives. We believe, as stated in an earlier chapter, that the best college education is one that produces a well-rounded individual who has a wide range of skills and interests. Even if you are focused on "getting that perfect job" after college and are fairly certain that you know what that job will be, investigating other fields and gathering skills and knowledge from various disciplines will make you a better professional in the long run, no matter what occupation or profession you finally choose.

You will, no doubt, encounter people who will tell you that becoming proficient in reading and writing will help you in any profession. In fact, many professionals tell us that being able to read critically and write well are valuable skills in any profession, and that good communication skills and the ability to think analytically are more important than academic knowledge learned in college. Still, even that is not enough reason to learn to communicate effectively. To that, we would add that the ability to communicate is what makes humans unique. In short, learning to read critically and write effectively will help you to become a better student, a better professional, and a better human being. Whether you are a person who is still unsure about your long-term professional goals or one who has felt a strong calling for a particular profession for many years, you can benefit from thinking, researching, reading, and writing about the possible professional and career paths you might take in the future.

THE GENRE—THE INFORMATIVE PROJECT

While we have primarily considered how to make arguments, writing is also a means of discovering what you think and feel about a subject and of communicating that discovery to the reader. Generally, this genre of writing is called informative writing. However, informative writing is much more than just providing information. You have probably already noticed that, as you write, you often begin to take a different direction from the one you had originally planned. Coming to different conclusions and changing your focus as you write or even after you have written the first draft is actually quite common. That is, as we have noted before, a part of how writing works. As you write, you often discover that you are beginning to feel very differently about that topic. Organizing your thoughts on paper and applying various narrative, analytical, and argumentative structures actually encourages you to discover new thinking and new ideas.

Often, this "journey" through the thought processes of the writer is what makes writing interesting and informative for the reader. After all, that is what good writers have to offer their readers. Writing is not just about stating a thesis and then supporting that thesis with interesting stories, insightful analysis, and sound argument. Writing is also about taking the reader on that journey as you discover what you think and feel about a topic.

Generally, almost all writing is informative as well as argumentative. After all, if you are to bring your stories, your analysis, and your argument to bear on a topic, then you are in some ways also informing the reader. While some people make a sharp distinction between "informative" and "argumentative" writing, the fact is that arguments also inform and all presentations of information are a form of argument. Even if you are writing a project that informs a reader how to download music from the Internet, you are still, in effect, arguing that your particular perspective on that process is a good or effective way to proceed. In writing that focuses primarily on providing information to the reader, the writer is still responsible for supplying appropriate *ethos*, *pathos*, and *logos*, and for supporting the argument that this information is credible, useful, pertinent, and up-to-date. To accomplish this, informative writing may also make use of narrative, analysis, and logic to interest the reader, to supply logical and emotional appeals, and to ensure that the reader feels that the information is credible.

Let us look at an essay from social critic Barbara Ehrenreich entitled "Premature Pragmatism."

> *The setting was one of those bucolic Ivy League campuses where the tuition exceeds the average American annual income and the favorite sport is white-water rafting--as far, in other words, as one might hope to get from the banal economic worries that plague the grown-up world. The subject, among the roomful of young women who had come*

to meet with me, turned to "life after college"—"if there is one" (nervous giggles). "My dream was to go into psychiatric social work," offered a serious young woman in overalls and a "Divest Now" button, "but I don't think I could live on that, so I'm going into banking instead." When I protested that she should hold on to her ideals and try to get by on the $30,000 or so a year psychiatric social workers earn, she looked baffled, as if I were recommending an internship with Mother Teresa.

"Ideals are all right when you're young," declared another woman, a campus activist who certainly seemed to fit the age group for which she found idealism appropriate, "but you do have to think of earning a living." Well, yes, I thought to myself, we older feminists have been saying for some time that the goal of higher education for women is not the "MRS" degree, but when did we ever say that it was banking?

Not that a little respect for the dollar isn't a fine thing in the young, and a useful antidote, in my day anyway, for the effects of too much Hesse or Kahlil Gibran. But no one in the room had gone so far as to suggest a career in almsgiving, washing lepers' feet, or doing literacy training among the Bushmen. "Idealism," to these undergraduates, was defined as an ordinary, respectable profession in the human services. "Realism" meant plunging almost straight from pubescence into the stone-hearted world of finance capitalism.

I call this mind-set, which you will find on almost any campus today, "premature pragmatism," and I am qualified to comment because I, too, was once a victim of it. I had gone to college with an intellectual agenda that included solving the mind-body problem, discovering the sources of human evil, and getting a tentative reading on the purpose of life. But within a few months I had dropped all that and become a chemistry major--partly because I had figured out that there were only meager rewards, in this world, for those who know the purpose of life and the source of all evil.

The result, twenty-odd years later, is more or less what you'd expect: I'm an ex-science major with no definite occupation (unless you count "writing," that universal cover for those who avoid wage slavery at all costs), and I am still obsessed by the Ultimate Questions, such as What It's All About and Whether the Universe Will Expand Forever. I could have turned out much worse; I could have stayed in chemistry and gone into something distinctly unidealistic like nerve gas or plastics, in which *case I might have become rich and would almost certainly also have become an embittered alcoholic or a middle-aged dropout. The point is that premature pragmatism didn't work for me, and I doubt that it will work for any young person intending to set aside a "Divest Now" button for one reading "You Have a Friend at Chase Manhattan."*

Yet premature pragmatism has become as popular on campuses as, in past eras, swallowing goldfish to impress one's friends or taking over the administration building to demand a better world. There has been a precipitous decline, just since the seventies, in the number of students majoring in mind-expanding but only incidentally remunerative fields like history and mathematics. Meanwhile, business--as an academic pursuit--is booming: almost one-fourth of all college graduates were business majors in 1983, compared to about one-seventh in 1973, while the proportions who major in philosophy or literature have vanished beyond the decimal point to less than 1 percent.

Even more alarming, to anyone whose own life has been scarred by premature pragmatism, is the decline in "idealism" as expressed by undergraduates and measured by pollsters. In 1968, 85 percent of college students said that they hoped their education would help them "develop a philosophy of life." In 1985, only 44 percent adhered to such lofty goals, while the majority expected that education would help them "earn a lot of money." There has been, in other words, almost a 50 percent decline in idealism and a 100 percent increase in venality, or to put it less judgmentally, premature pragmatism.

I concede, though, that there are good reasons for the hard-nosed pragmatism of today's college students. They face rougher times, economically, than did my generation or the generation before mine. As economists Frank Levy and Richard Michel have recently shown, today's baby boomers (and especially the younger ones) are far less likely than their own parents to be able to buy a home, maintain a family on one income, or to watch their standard of living improve as they grow older.

So the best comeback for the young woman in overalls would have been for her to snap at me, "You think I should live on thirty thousand dollars a year! Well, perhaps you hadn't noticed that the National Association of Homebuilders now estimates that it takes an income of thirty-seven thousand dollars a year to be able to afford a modest, median-priced home. Or that if I want to send my own eventual children to a college like this I will need well over fifty thousand dollars a year. Or are you suggesting that I rely on a rich husband?" And she would have been dead on the mark: in today's economy, idealism is a luxury that most of us are likely to enjoy only at the price of simple comforts like housing and education. The mood on campus isn't so much venality as it is fear.

But still, premature pragmatism isn't necessarily a winning strategy. In the first place, what looks like "realism" at age eighteen may become sheer folly by age thirty-eight. Occupations go in and out of corporate favor, so that chemistry, for example--which seemed to be a safe bet two decades ago--has become one of those disciplines that prepare people for a life in the retail end of the newspaper business. The same may eventually happen to today's campus favorites--like law, management, and finance. At least it seems to me that there must be an ecological limit to the number of paper pushers the earth can sustain, and that human civilization will collapse when the number of, say, tax lawyers exceeds the world's total population of farmers, weavers, fisherpersons, and pediatric nurses.

Furthermore, with any luck at all, one becomes a rather different person at age thirty-eight than one was at eighteen. The list of famous people who ended up in a different line of work than the one they first embarked on includes Clark Gable (former lumberjack), artist Henri Rousseau (postal clerk), Elvis Presley (truck driver), St. Augustine (playboy), Walt Disney (ambulance driver), and Che Guevara (physician). Heads of state are notoriously ill prepared for their mature careers; think of Adolf Hitler (landscape painter), Ho Chi Minh (seaman), and our own Ronald Reagan. Women's careers are if anything even more unpredictable, to judge from my own friends: Barbara (a biochemist turned novelist), Sara (French literature professor, now a book editor), cousin Barb (anthropology to medicine).

But the saddest thing about today's premature pragmatists is not that they will almost certainly be unprepared for their mid-life career destinations, but that they will be unprepared for Life, in the grand sense, at all. The years between eighteen and twenty-two were not given to us to be frittered away in contemplation of future tax shelters and mortgage payments. In fact, it is almost a requirement of developmental biology that these years be spent in erotic reverie, metaphysical speculation, and schemes for universal peace and justice. Sometimes, of course, we lose sight of the heroic dreams of youth later on, as overdue bills and carburetor problems take their toll. But those who never dream at all start to lose much more--their wit, empathy, perspective, and, for lack of a more secular term, their immortal souls.

Then what about the fact that it takes nearly a six-figure income to achieve what used to be known as a "middle-class" lifestyle? What about my young Ivy League friend, forced to choose between a career in human service and what she believes, perhaps realistically, to be an adequate income? All I can say is that there is something grievously wrong with a culture that values Wall Street sharks above social workers, armament manufacturers above artists, or, for that matter, corporate lawyers above homemakers. Somehow, we're going to have to make the world a little more habitable for idealists, whether they are eighteen or thirty-eight. In fact, I suspect that more and more young people, forced to choose between their ideals and their economic security, will start opting instead for a career in social change. "The pay is lousy," as veteran writer-historian-social-change-activist Irving Howe likes to say, "but it's steady work."

Ehrenriech's essay is informative, but the information is surrounded by interesting narrative, trenchant analysis, and a provocative argument. Rather than simply supplying the reader with facts and statistics designed to present information about the process of choosing a career path, she opens with a narrative about her visit to the college classroom that is full of vivid description and dialogue and that grabs our attention and keeps us interested. In the section that follows, she works to establish her ethos as one who has been "a victim" of what she calls "premature pragmatism," a term that she cleverly designs to present her argument.

Notice that Ehrenriech is careful to consider what the objections to her argument might be, as she freely admits that today's college students "face rougher times." Including a discussion of possible objections to her argument only serves to increase her credibility. Still, the fact that she considers those objections does not cause her to abandon her point: that "premature pragmatism" is a bad idea. The information—statistics about trends in college majors, the changing need for various professionals, the economic prospects for the future, and the previous professions of famous people and personal friends—is used to make an argument and is presented in a way that is focused on the values her ideal community of readers (college students) might share. The essay is carefully crafted to inform and to persuade and includes appropriate appeals to *ethos, pathos,* and *logos.*

A *Activity*

Ehrenriech is noted for the use of humor and sarcasm in her essays. Can you locate places in the essay where she attempts to inject a bit of humor? How well does this element work in the essay and how does it serve to make the information that she presents less "dry?"

THE IDEAL COMMUNITY OF READERS FOR THE INFORMATIVE PROJECT

When thinking about your ideal community of readers for the informative essay, it is extremely important to begin with an idea of what the imagined reader might already know and not know about the subject. You can never be sure that everything in your informative essay will be new information for the reader, of course, but you can concentrate your informative writing on what you think might be unknown to your readers or on dispelling misconceptions about the subject. To achieve this, you might concentrate on what you, yourself, discovered about your topic as you researched, planned, or wrote.

Too often, informative writing becomes dry and uninteresting because writers have not thoroughly considered the ideal community of readers for the information. An informative writing is much more than just a presentation of information. Information must be presented with a clear idea of who will be reading the informative writing, how they might make use of that information, and what they might expect when they encounter information on the topic. Often, what is interesting about informative writing is that it presents information that is new to most readers. However, good informative writing can also use familiar information to dispel readers' misconceptions or to make new connections with fresh analysis. Exigency and readership are still primary concerns for informative writing, and you can begin to establish the "situation" for your informative writing by asking the following questions:

❏ What kind of readers will likely be interested in the information and why?

❏ What will these readers probably already know about the subject and what misconceptions might they have about the topic?

❏ What values might this ideal community of readers share and how can I focus my presentation in a way that appeals to those values in order to make the information more useful and to make the writing more interesting?

❏ How can I present myself as a credible source for this information?

By carefully considering whom the ideal community of readers might be for your informative writing, you can determine what the readers might already know or think they know, and you can present the elements of information that they might find useful. Establishing the ideal community of readers will allow you to make choices about what kinds of information to present and, more importantly, why.

 Activity

Imagine that you are designing an informative writing about an activity in which you participate or a hobby you have (surfing, coin collecting, chess, tennis, playing guitar, running, horseback riding, etc.). How would an informative writing be different for an ideal community of readers that also participated in that activity or hobby from one for readers who had never participated? How would that change the purpose of the writing? The topic? The types of information presented? The focus of the information? The type of narrative and argument you might make in the writing?

THE TOPICS FOR THE INFORMATIVE PROJECT

The purpose of your informative writing is tied to the ideal community of readers for your writing. By considering what those readers might already know and how they might use the information you can establish how "in depth" the information needs to be and on what parts of the information you need to concentrate. An informative writing is much more than just a collection of what you already know about a subject or what you can find out by researching. By focusing first on who the ideal community of readers might be and what purpose these readers might have for your information, you can avoid simply recounting everything that you know or can find out. Often, the ideal situation is to imagine what misconceptions readers might have about the subject. You might begin by asking yourself what misconceptions you had.

THE PROBLEM APPROACH AND THE INFORMATIVE PROJECT

As you are selecting a topic and planning for your informative project, keep in mind that you will also be making an argument. Whether you are conscious of it or not, your selection of topic and your presentation of information presents an argument for your perspective on the profession. You will be wise, then, to consciously plan for that argument. Think of it this way: the "problem" is that your readers do not know enough about the profession or that the readers have misconceptions about the profession.

❏ Is this a significant problem that deserves our attention? Your job in presenting information to readers is to make them appreciate the importance of that information.

❏ Why is this profession important at all? Why is it important for you? Is it important that you clear up misconceptions about the profession? Why?

❏ How big a problem is it? Here, you can indicate just how important this profession is and why people need to know more about it. Why do readers need to know more about this profession?

❏ How did it get to be a problem? If you chose to focus on this aspect of the problem approach, you could write about the history of the profession or why and how it became more important. You might also write about how misconceptions about the field came to be common.

❏ What will happen if we fail to address the problem? You might write about the future of the profession or about what will happen if misconceptions about the profession persist.

❏ What can be done about the problem? Are there benefits of knowing more about this profession for the reader? Might the reader be more appreciative of the profession or understand it better? Might the reader be interested in joining the profession or in offering some other type of support?

THE TOULMIN METHOD AND THE INFORMATIVE PROJECT

For the informative project, your **claim** (the purpose of your argument) could be that because of your desire to help children reach their full potential you have chosen to become a middle-school teacher. The **grounds** (the basic facts) for that claim might be that teachers do, in fact, help children reach their potential. The **warrants** (the major supporting points) would be everything from narratives about how you developed your desire to help children reach their potential to the details of how to become a teacher or what teachers actually do. The **backing**, as always, is the details of those warrants. **Qualifiers** and **rebuttals** could include issues such as the fact that not everyone is suited to the profession or that there are variations in what kind of training teachers need or arguments that the rewards of the profession are not necessarily monetary.

POSSIBILITIES FOR NARRATIVE IN THE INFORMATIVE PROJECT

Narrative structures can establish your credibility to present the information in your project or to establish what purpose the information might serve. You might consider adding a narrative about how you became interested in the subject of your informative project, how you researched the information, or how you will use the information. If you feel that you do not yet know enough about the subject, then a narrative structure could improve your *ethos* by demonstrating that you are in the process of gathering knowledge and putting that knowledge to good use. You do not have to be an expert on a subject to write an informative piece; you only have to be interested and resourceful. Above all, adding a narrative structure to your informative writing can help keep the information from becoming dry and uninteresting.

POSSIBILITIES FOR ANALYSIS IN THE INFORMATIVE PROJECT

Choosing what information to present in an informative project is only part of the effort. You will need to suggest what the information means, at least to you. As always, what readers will be looking for is your analysis. Simply presenting information is not enough. In fact, all informative writing is really a form of analysis, no matter how objective the author tries to be. What you discovered or know about the subject is colored by your own experiences and processed through your own mind. Bringing that experience or those thought processes into the writing will allow your readers to evaluate the information for themselves and to decide if and how they might use the information. Writing about your own misconceptions, analyzing why you had them, and revealing how the information served to dispel those misconceptions will strengthen your *ethos* and supply some of the analysis. What is important is that you make the processes by which you discovered the information and your interpretation of that information obvious and interesting. Writing an informative piece requires more than doing the research for the reader; it also requires that you present your analysis of that information. Otherwise, readers would be better served by just going through the process of discovery for themselves. Be sure to add what you think the information means and to suggest how the information might be useful to the reader.

POSSIBILITIES FOR ARGUMENT IN THE INFORMATIVE PROJECT

As all informative writing is a form of analysis, it is also a form of argument. Even if you are simply presenting information, you are still arguing that the information you are presenting is valid, useful, and complete for the purpose of the writing. As such, you will still want to employ the appeals of *ethos*, *pathos*, and *logos*. Your narrative structures, your analytical structures, and your logical structures must demonstrate why the reader should find you a credible source of information and why your information might be valuable. Leaving out important parts of the information, not addressing what your readers might already know, leaving misconceptions unaddressed, interpreting the information incorrectly, or not interpreting the information at all will all make your informative writing less effective and damage your credibility. You will, as always, be searching for values that your ideal community of readers might share and adjusting your argument to appeal to those values. Ask yourself what makes your information valuable to your ideal community of readers by considering what information your readers might value. In informative writing, you are arguing that your information is valid and the information is useful to your ideal community of readers.

A Vocational Informative Project

In this chapter, you learned that the choice of a possible vocation can be based not only on the desire to make money but on personal convictions and experiences as well. For this project, you will report on an investigation you conduct about a vocation or profession that you might choose to follow once you complete your college education. You might include your personal reasons for considering this particular vocation in order to give your ideal community of readers an idea of why someone might consider entering this profession. In addition, you might include a section in which you dispel some of the common myths that people might have about this profession and include some information about ways that people might engage in this profession in ways they might not already know about. In order to help you collect information for the project, complete some research suggested by the blog assignments below.

1. **Prewriting**: Complete a short passage for your blog from one of the following research projects:

   A. Interview several classmates to find out what they know and assume about this profession. For example, if you are investigating the possibility of a job in the medical field, in teaching, or in public relations, ask people what they know about these professions and what they think people in these professions actually do. You might also ask them what they know about how much and what kind of training a person needs for this profession, and what kind of personal and monetary benefits a professional in this field can expect. Make a list of these assumptions and ideas and write a short summary of how most people view the profession. If you have access to a camera, you may want to film these interviews and, with permission of the interviewees, create a video blog.

   B. Interview a professional in the field you have chosen and ask them how much training they had in college and how that training served them after they entered the profession. Ask them how their expectations for the job compare to the actual day-to-day performance of their jobs.

   C. Starting with the Bureau of Labor Statistics website, conduct a short investigation of the possible future need for people in the profession you have chosen to investigate. You will also likely be able to find more articles and websites on the "top jobs" for future graduates on the web, in your school's counseling center. You can also get some help in this research by asking the reference librarian in your school library for help and by asking professionals in the field. Using what information you can find, prepare a short report with links about the top jobs and, if possible, the future need for people in the field you have chosen.

2. **Drafting**: Before you begin to draft, complete the Checklist of Questions for Establishing Exigency (p. 44) and the Checklist of Questions for Structure (p. 67). Check your classmates' blogs and consider what made their blog posts work well or what they might have done better so that you can apply those lessons to your project.

   Narrative: For this project, your personal narrative about why you became interested in this profession or vocation might be a good place to begin your project. You might recount the event or events that caused you to first become interested in this field as a way to establish some credibility for the project. You might also recount the work you did on your blog project to provide a narrative to frame the information that you gathered from your research.

   Analysis: Your analysis of the information you have gathered about the profession for your blog entry might be important for this project. The idea is to inform your reader about the profession, and so your analysis of the information is of primary importance. Although the project is primarily informative, it is important that you present your analysis of that information. While readers will, of course, be free to interpret the information for themselves, you are also required to synthesize all the information in a way that makes sense, or meaning.

   Argument: While this project is primarily informational, you will still be making a sort of argument in the project. While you may not be going so far as to try to persuade someone to consider entering the profession you have chosen to research, you will still be making an argument that your interpretation of the information is a valid one. In short, your presentation of the information must still make logical sense. The conclusions you make about the profession, its future, and its actual demands and rewards must be supported by the information and by your analysis.

3. **Peer Review**: After you complete the first draft, submit your draft for peer review and complete the peer review questionnaires for your classmate

4. **The Visual**: Select an appropriate visual image to accompany your project. Complete the Checklist of Questions for Visuals (p. 204) and consider carefully how the visual will support your argument.

5. **Revision and Proofing**: After you have selected your visual, completed your peer reviews, and received your peer-reviewed draft back, make revisions, and check your sentences. Check your work against the Checklist of Questions for Process (p. 27). As always, you will want to read your final draft aloud before you consider it complete. After you are confident of your revision and proofing, save your file. Follow the instructions for uploading the project.

PEER REVIEW QUESTIONNAIRE FOR THE VOCATIONAL INFORMATIVE PROJECT

Your Name:

Title of the essay you are peer reviewing:

Author of the essay:

Answer the following questions about the project you are reviewing in a complete sentence or in a short paragraph.

1. Summarize three of the major pieces of information that you gathered from the essay. These might include the reason or reasons that the writer became interested in the profession, what future prospects exist for the profession, and what the realities of the profession are:

2. Describe what you like most about the essay you are reviewing:

3. Did you have any misconceptions about the profession that were dispelled by the writer? What were those misconceptions and what did you learn?

4. Pick your favorite sentence from the project and copy it here. Then describe what you like about the sentence:

5. If the writer has included a visual image with the project, how do you think the visual adds to the project? Does it seem appropriate to the project? Does it contribute to the project? How? Could you suggest a more useful or appropriate visual for the project?

CHAPTER EIGHT

MAKING ACADEMIC CHOICES: WRITING AN ACADEMIC SYNTHESIS PROJECT

> "With a little more deliberation in the choice of their pursuits, all men would perhaps become essentially students and observers, for certainly their nature and destiny are interesting to all alike"
>
> --Henry David Thoreau

THE SITUATION

While you are in college, you will, no doubt, be called on to read critically and to analyze texts in most of your other classes, and many of those classes will also require you to write papers or to respond to essay questions as part of the coursework. In fact, teachers in every field increasingly employ writing assignments to help students learn, to familiarize them with various academic discourse communities, and to test their knowledge of the material being covered. Even some math teachers now assign writing to help their students grasp concepts and to test their ability to communicate those concepts effectively. Your literature, history, psychology, engineering, education, and science classes will all probably require you to write as part of the coursework, and we are certain that being able to write in ways that emphasize a consideration of audience, structure, and argument will make you a more effective and successful student. In addition to helping you complete your writing assignments in your coursework, your knowledge of how authors use rhetoric will help you read critically as well. Just as professionals value graduates that can read and communicate effectively, so, too, do teachers in all disciplines look for students who can analyze and think about what they read and who can write and communicate that knowledge effectively.

In fact, the writing that you do in your academic career will indubitably test your ability to analyze how the various discourse communities that make up the university employ genres, considerations of readership, argument structures, and conventions of style and formatting. While the writing conventions may be somewhat similar across the disciplines, there are also important differences in what readers expect within the various discourse communities of the academic disciplines. Still, the common threads of rhetoric will also be apparent if you look for them. Aristotle believed that rhetoric was, in fact, a sort of "master discipline," and that an effective grasp of how arguments are constructed would allow the skilled communicator to succeed in understanding and creating original arguments on almost any topic.

In fact, when you are asked to write a paper or answer an essay question in your classes, your first step should be to ask the same sorts of questions you have asked about the projects you have written for this course. One of the keys to a successful academic career is realizing how much the knowledge you gain in each of your classes can be used in your other classes, and most teachers consider that reading critically and writing effectively are abilities that students should demonstrate in all their coursework. If you employ the knowledge you have gained to read carefully, and if you make conscious choices about genre, readership, structure, and style as you write in your other classes, you will be a more effective student.

Academic writing requires that you analyze the conventions of writing in the discipline in which you are writing so that you write in ways that readers in that discipline will recognize and respond to. You history professor will not expect you to write like a historian without some help and instruction, but he or she will expect that you already know how to read critically and write with a consideration of purpose and readership.

THE GENRE—THE SYNTHESIS PROJECT

Academic writing is one of the most misunderstood genres of writing. Often, students believe that writing for class is really just another way that professors test students on the specific knowledge they have learned in lectures or by reading textbooks. Academic writing is more than that, though. In reality, academic writing is often a synthesis of many genres: it contains narrative, opinion, critique, and informative writing to make an argument.

Students sometimes believe that the lessons they learn about rhetoric and writing in their writing classes only apply to their writing classes. Generally, all your professors expect that your writing will be skillfully done, that it will contain careful and original analysis and argument, that it will show a basic understanding of how knowledge is communicated in the specific discipline, and that it also demonstrates understanding of the course content. That is, of course, a very difficult list of things to accomplish, and it is hard to blame professors for not having the time to teach discipline-specific writing conventions along with course content. Instead, they expect that students have attended writing classes where they have been taught to analyze rhetoric effectively as they read and that students use that ability in all their classes. Your history professor may never mention that the conventions of writing about history are slightly different than the conventions of writing about biology. More than likely, though, both history and biology professors will expect that students read history and biology texts with an eye toward learning how the discourse conventions work and that the students employ some of those conventions in the projects they write for their classes. Still, whatever the discipline, the genre of academic writing requires that students demonstrate ability to present information, to analyze and critique texts, to make arguments that are designed for a specific community of readers, and to synthesize everything within their own experiences.

In other words, academic writing makes use of all the abilities you have learned by writing in all varieties of genres. Whether you have been assigned to write a full research paper with an original argument and original research or you are merely writing the answer to an essay question, the genre of academic writing requires you to make use of the ability to employ the narrative, analytical, and argument structures that you have learned in this course. Academic writing also requires you to consider the purpose of your writing and that you write for a community of readers. However, you do not have to imagine an ideal community of readers for your academic writing. In this case, the community of readers is made up of people who study and write in that discipline. As such, readers will expect that a history paper looks and sounds like a history paper, that a lab report for a biology class looks and sounds like a lab report, and that a business proposal for a management class looks and sounds like a business report that a manager (or at least a student in a management course) would write. All of these different forms of academic writing demand that you write with a sense of purpose and that you employ effective rhetoric—including a sense of readership that demonstrates at least basic understanding of what the specific academic discourse community values.

THE IDEAL COMMUNITY OF READERS FOR THE ACADEMIC PROJECT

The ideal community of readers for the academic project consists of other readers and writers in that field. As we have noted, there is a way to write "for the professor" and still have a sense of readership in your writing. After all, your professor is an actual member of the discourse community of that discipline and so is also a member of the ideal community of readers for your academic writing. This makes it both easier and harder to produce effective academic writing--easier because you know a member of the ideal community of readers for your text, harder because you must make sure that you meet the expectations of a member of that discourse community, or at least the expectations that a member would have for a student project.

There are at least four ways that students can address the difficulty of writing academic papers:

- ❏ First, take advantage of your assigned readings and your professor's lectures to analyze how words are used, how sources are employed, how arguments are generally made, and how structures of narrative, analysis, and argument are generally employed in the discipline. This will be difficult to remember, as you go to lectures and read primarily to learn the content. Still, use the rhetorical skills you have learned to notice how rhetoric is used in the various discourse communities of the academic world and try to use those conventions in your academic writing.

- ❏ Second, take advantage of your access to the professor, a bona fide member of the academic discourse community, to ask questions about how to construct effective academic writing within that discipline. Almost all professors will be glad to share this information with you.

- ❏ Third, take advantage of the fact that you will be surrounded by other students. Unless your professor specifically forbids it, have the other students read your work and read theirs. Ask them what they have noticed about academic writing in that discipline and make use of your peer reviewing skills.

- ❏ Fourth, remember what you have learned about writing and rhetoric and apply it to all your academic writing.

There is one constant in all effective writing: good rhetorical skills, good writing habits, peer reviewing skills, and an awareness of readership.

THE TOPICS FOR THE ACADEMIC PROJECT

For this project, you will produce a piece of academic writing that explains to the reader how your academic discipline has value beyond the academic setting. Usually, academic writing requires you to make original, researched arguments about something within the field, or it asks that you report on information you have learned. As you are probably new to your disciplinary field, however, we want you to think and write about how one specific academic discipline addresses a problem in the community, the nation, or the world. As such, the project calls for you to write for a more general audience to inform them about the chosen discipline and to argue the field's significance to the local, national, or global community. Still, you should try to employ some of the disciplinary conventions of writing for that field.

As we have suggested, going to college is not just about training you for the job market. In our democracy, it is expected that each of us contribute to the general welfare of the community, the nation, and the world, and so academic work is valued not just because it trains you to be a teacher, a doctor, a businessperson, or an engineer but because, in order to function, our communities need skilled experts in these fields. It is easy to see how some professions contribute to the general good. Teachers, doctors, nurses, engineers, bio-chemists, physical therapists, and journalists all do work that will obviously make the community and the world better. The idea is, though, that all who are trained for the professions will contribute their knowledge and expertise to make the world around us a better place.

The question that should guide your academic project is "what specific problems and issues does your chosen discipline address and how does it produce knowledge and expertise from which we all benefit?" If you have not yet chosen an academic field of study, this project represents a chance for you to investigate an academic discipline and its relevance. After all, the possibility of monetary reward is only one reason for choosing a field of study. Knowing that you are contributing to society is often more rewarding than simply working to pay your bills, buying expensive cars and houses, or storing up huge piles of cash. Part of the personal satisfaction of learning an academic discipline is in knowing that you are a contributing member of society and that your work produces something of tangible benefit to others.

Following is a short justification for studying history written by Peter N. Stearns and taken from the website of the American Historical Association:

> *People live in the present. They plan for and worry about the future. History, however, is the study of the past. Given all the demands that press in from living in the present and anticipating what is yet to come, why bother with what has been? Given all the desirable and available branches of knowledge, why insist—as most American educational programs do—on a good bit of history? And why urge many students to study even more history than they are required to?*
>
> *Any subject of study needs justification: its advocates must explain why it is worth attention. Most widely accepted subjects—and history is certainly one of them—attract some people who simply like the information and modes of thought involved. But audiences less*

spontaneously drawn to the subject and more doubtful about why to bother need to know what the purpose is.

Historians do not perform heart transplants, improve highway design, or arrest criminals. In a society that quite correctly expects education to serve useful purposes, the functions of history can seem more difficult to define than those of engineering or medicine. History is in fact very useful, actually indispensable, but the products of historical study are less tangible, sometimes less immediate, than those that stem from some other disciplines.

In the past history has been justified for reasons we would no longer accept. For instance, one of the reasons history holds its place in current education is because earlier leaders believed that a knowledge of certain historical facts helped distinguish the educated from the uneducated; the person who could reel off the date of the Norman conquest of England (1066) or the name of the person who came up with the theory of evolution at about the same time that Darwin did (Wallace) was deemed superior—a better candidate for law school or even a business promotion. Knowledge of historical facts has been used as a screening device in many societies, from China to the United States, and the habit is still with us to some extent. Unfortunately, this use can encourage mindless memorization—a real but not very appealing aspect of the discipline.

History should be studied because it is essential to individuals and to society, and because it harbors beauty. There are many ways to discuss the real functions of the subject—as there are many different historical talents and many different paths to historical meaning. All definitions of history's utility, however, rely on two fundamental facts.

History Helps Us Understand People and Societies

In the first place, history offers a storehouse of information about how people and societies behave. Understanding the operations of people and societies is difficult, though a number of disciplines make the attempt. An exclusive reliance on current data would needlessly handicap our efforts. How can we evaluate war if the nation is at peace—unless we use historical materials? How can we understand genius, the influence of technological innovation, or the role that beliefs play in shaping family life, if we don't use what we know about experiences in the past? Some social scientists attempt to formulate laws or theories about human behavior. But even these recourses depend on historical information, except for in limited, often artificial cases in which experiments can be devised to determine how people act. Major aspects of a society's operation, like mass elections, missionary activities, or military alliances, cannot be set up as precise experiments. Consequently, history must serve, however imperfectly, as our laboratory, and data from the past must serve as our most vital evidence in the unavoidable quest to figure out why our complex species behaves as it does in societal settings. This, fundamentally, is why we cannot stay away from history: it offers the only extensive evidential base for the contemplation and analysis of how societies function, and people need to have some sense of how societies function simply to run their own lives.

History Helps Us Understand Change and How the Society We Live in Came to Be

The second reason history is inescapable as a subject of serious study follows closely on the first. The past causes the present, and so the future. Any time we try to know why something happened—whether a shift in political party dominance in the American Congress, a major change in the teenage suicide rate, or a war in the Balkans or the Middle East—we have to look for factors that took shape earlier. Sometimes fairly recent history will suffice to explain a major development, but often we need to look further back to identify the causes of change. Only through studying history can we grasp how things change; only through history can we begin to comprehend the factors that cause change; and only through history can we understand what elements of an institution or a society persist despite change.

Papers such as this one are easily found for almost every discipline. We suggest that you do some research on the discipline you have chosen by finding some of these on your own in order to begin to plan for this project. One way to find these is to visit the academic department in your chosen field or to look up the associations that members of this disciplinary field belong to. Remember, though, that your project should contain your analysis of this discipline's value to the community, and these documents are merely places to start your thinking.

THE PROBLEM APPROACH TO THE ACADEMIC PROJECT

Although this project will include much information, you will be arguing for the value of your academic discipline to our culture. As such, you could deploy the problem approach to help you plan that argument.

❏ Is this a significant problem that deserves our attention? We suggest for this project that this is a key question, since the project will be arguing for the value, the significance, of your discipline.

❏ How big a problem is it? Some disciplines, such as nursing or teaching, might seem to offer more intrinsic value than others. Nevertheless, if you work to provide an answer to this question, you may find that your discipline addresses very important issues that others do not or that it addresses issues in very specific and beneficial ways.

❏ How did it get to be a problem? Here you might write about the history of your discipline or the history of your discipline's work with whatever issues your discipline is addressing.

❏ What will happen if we fail to address the problem? This question points to the future of your discipline and its importance. What is that future and how will it change with future needs? Will your discipline become more important? Why?

❏ What can be done about the problem? You might consider addressing the specific solutions your discipline offers for specific problems and how those solutions might be implemented.

THE TOULMIN METHOD AND THE ACADEMIC PROJECT

If you choose to use the Toulmin method to help you design your academic essay, you might consider a **claim** (the purpose for your argument) like teachers serve an important function in society because they teach students about diverse cultures. The **grounds** (the basic facts) for such a claim might be that teachers do, in fact, teach students about diverse cultures. The **warrants** (the major supporting points) would be all the information about how teachers teach students about diverse cultures and arguments in support of the idea that this is an important function they provide for society. The **backing** would be the details of those warrants. **Qualifiers** and **rebuttals** might include items such as the fact that other institutions and disciplines also serve this function or that this is only one of many functions of teachers, etc.

POSSIBILITIES FOR NARRATIVE IN THE ACADEMIC PROJECT

One of the ways to avoid letting your research "take over" your project is to include narrative structures. You might want to include a story that highlights the beginnings of your interest in this disciplinary field, or you might include a narrative that describes some of the research you did for the project. As with the project on making vocational choices, you can include narratives about the misconceptions that you or others have about the importance of your chosen academic discipline. You might write about someone else who has chosen this field of study and add a narrative about their interest in the discipline or about their activities. Above all, adding a narrative will personalize your project and give you some information to write about other than what you find in your research.

POSSIBILITIES FOR ANALYSIS IN THE ACADEMIC PROJECT

As with all your projects, your analysis of the information will be the key element that makes your project unique. Avoid simply reporting what others have said about the importance of your discipline to the general community. Your analysis of the narratives and the information will be what your reader will want to read. As always, it is up to you to make meaning from the information, to provide the interpretation of the narratives, the opinions, the facts, and the statistics. As we have noted, this project will ask you to synthesize the work in various genres that you have done. You can provide your narrative and analyze what it means; you can offer your opinion about how your discipline addresses issues or about the value of your discipline to society, you will, of course be informing your readers about your discipline, but you will be synthesizing all this within an analytical format.

POSSIBILITIES FOR ARGUMENT IN THE ACADEMIC PROJECT

In the end, you will be making an argument that the field you have chosen to write about contributes in some way to the overall good of the community. While readers may not run to the history department to become a history major after reading your project, they will gain an understanding that the study of your chosen disciplinary field is important to the general welfare of your community, the nation, or the world. Or your readers might at least accept your argument that your chosen discipline is right for you and that it serves your desire to study or consider studying in that discipline.

AN ACADEMIC SYNTHESIS PROJECT

In this chapter, we examined the intersection of the academic disciplines with cultural and social issues. As was discussed, each academic discipline at least partially justifies its study by highlighting just what that study contributes to the general benefit of individuals, the local community, and the world. For this project, you will produce an essay that explains the importance of an academic discipline to a "lay" reader, that explains the major area of study for that academic discipline, and that relates that study to a current problem faced by individuals, the community, or the world. For example, your essay might examine how the field of psychology addresses current questions of drug abuse, obesity, or mental disease in your community, the nation, or the world. Or, you might examine how the field of criminal justice is developing new techniques of forensics to help solve crime or new ideas about the penal system. Or, your project might examine how the field of literary studies is addressing new questions about what it means to be literate in a technological age.

Your over-all goal is to explain to the reader just exactly what people who work in a specific discipline study and how that study benefits society.

1. **Prewriting**: In this chapter, you learned how academic disciplines define themselves based on a shared set of values and a shared discourse. As a prewriting exercise, conduct an interview with a faculty member from your chosen discipline that focuses on what problems that discipline is currently addressing and how the discipline is attempting to address those problems. You might also find and visit several of the professional association websites for the discipline to examine these issues, and you could also find an introductory textbook for your chosen discipline and read through the opening chapter. After you have completed your interview, visited the website, and read the chapter from the textbook, complete a short passage for your blog from one of the following ideas:

    A. Write a short report on the interview you conducted, highlighting one major problem that your chosen discipline is addressing and how the discipline is attempting to address that issue.

    B. Write a short reaction to the professional website you visited, describing the major parts of the website and what important issues the website highlights for the discipline.

C. Come up with what you think are the three biggest misconceptions about your chosen discipline and "debunk" those misconceptions in a short blog entry.

2. **Drafting**: Before you begin to draft, complete the Checklist of Questions for Establishing Exigency (p. 44) and the Checklist of Questions for Structure. (p. 67) Check your classmates' blogs and consider what made their blog posts work well or what they might have done better so that you can apply those lessons to your project. Draft an essay that begins with a brief narrative about how you became interested in the discipline you have chosen. Then include a section that examines some of the major ideas, areas of study, tenets, and theories used by people in your chosen discipline. Then, include a section that explains how work in your chosen discipline addresses a problem in your community or the world. Use appropriate quotes, summaries, and paraphrasing from your interview, the website, and your reading in your essay, and cite the material you use as outlined in the appendix on research. As always, carefully consider what you will analyze in your essay and what you will argue about:

Narrative: For the narrative section of your essay, you might want to highlight how you became interested in the academic discipline that you have chosen and how you might use your study in that discipline to improve things in your community or in the world. There might be one specific experience that sparked your interest in the academic discipline you might choose to study, or your interest might be based on a series of events that led to your interest.

Analysis: It is important that you explain to the reader the connection between your personal interests and the discipline, just what it is that your chosen discipline studies, and what problems and issues in the community and the world the discipline is attempting to address. Part of your goal is to make your reader understand why someone would be interested in studying in your chosen discipline, to explain what your chosen discipline does and is concerned with, and to examine how your chosen discipline intersects with community or global issues.

Argument: In this project, you are basically arguing for the importance of your chosen discipline to the community and the world. Your goal is to convince the reader that your chosen discipline has importance for these communities. You will also be constructing an argument that there are sound reasons to be interested in the discipline, that the issues your chosen discipline addresses are important, and that the discipline is developing some possible answers for those issues.

3. **Peer Review**: After you complete the first draft, send it to your blog partners for peer review and peer review their first drafts, completing the peer review questionnaire for the project.

4. **The Visual**: Select an appropriate visual image to accompany your essay. Complete the Checklist of Questions for Visuals (p. 204) and consider carefully how the visual will support your argument. You might choose a photo of an important figure in your discipline, someone engaged in the practice of your discipline, or an appropriate symbol from a professional association's website.

5. **Revision and Proofing**: After you have selected your visual, completed your peer reviews, and received your peer-reviewed draft back, make revisions, and check your sentences. Check your work against the Checklist of Questions for Process (p. 27). As always, you will want to read your final draft aloud before you consider it complete. After you are confident of your revision and proofing, save your file. Follow the instructions for uploading the project.

Peer Review Questionnaire for the Academic Synthesis Project

Your Name:

Title of the essay you are peer reviewing:

Author of the essay:

Answer the following questions about the project you are reviewing in a complete sentence or in a short paragraph.

1. Summarize the problem in the main point of the project. What problem in the local, national, or global community does the writer say that people in the academic discipline are trying to address?

2. Describe what you like most about the essay you are reviewing:

3. What was the most interesting thing you learned from reading the project?

4. Pick your favorite sentence from the project and copy it here. Then describe what you like about the sentence:

5. If the writer has included a visual image with the project, how do you think the visual adds to the project? Does it seem appropriate to the project? Does it contribute to the project? How? Could you suggest a more useful or appropriate visual for the project?

THE REFLECTIVE PROJECT

Throughout the projects you have completed for this course, you have been asked to consider more carefully the choices that are available to you as you write. In each project, we have asked that you imagine the situation for your writing more fully so that you may effectively employ rhetoric to help you construct writing that might actually influence an ideal community of readers. Each project has asked that you learn to use narrative, analysis, and argumentative structures to communicate your purpose more effectively and to make choices about how your writing works based on a clear understand of the rhetorical situation for that writing.

In order for this course to be effective, however, you must remember to use these techniques even after you have completed this course. As such, it will be important for you to take what you have learned in this course and apply it to all the writing situations you encounter in the academic world and in your professional and personal life. The temptation will be to revert to writing for the teacher, at least in your academic writing. We ask that you remember to more fully consider the situation for your writing. We believe that by considering the situation for each project that you write in the future—whether that is for a class, for a job, or in your personal life—you will increase your writing ability and communicate more effectively.

The first step in carrying this new knowledge and ability forward is to review the things you have learned and to examine how your writing has changed. The goal of this project will be to review the projects you have completed, to examine the peer review questionnaires you have received from your classmates, and to look over the comments that your teacher has made about your work to reflect on what you have learned about writing and discover how your writing has changed. By examining your work, you can begin to determine what skills and abilities you have now as a writer, what skills and abilities you still need to work on, and set some goals for yourself in your future writing projects.

For this project, you will produce a reflective project that examines the differences in your initial attitudes about writing and how those attitudes have changed, that highlights your achievements in the course, that looks at what progress you have made, and that sets goals for future writing projects.

1. **Prewriting**: For each project you have completed, you have answered two sets of questions before writing, the Checklist of Questions for Establishing Exigency (p. 44) and Checklist of Questions for Structure (p. 67). You have also collected Peer Review Questionnaires for each project and received a response and grade from your teacher. Read through all those documents and use your analytical skills to construct a blog entry that answers the following questions:

   A. How have your attitudes about writing changed from the beginning to the end of this course? How important do you feel talent is to becoming a competent writer now? When reading your literacy narrative now, do you feel that any of your attitudes toward writing have changed? What is the best piece of advice you could give to a student just beginning this course?

   B. Which project seemed to produce the best writing for you? Why do you think that is?

   C. What is the most important thing you learned from reading your classmates' projects for peer review? How have you incorporated that lesson into your own writing?

2. **Drafting**: Before you begin to draft your reflective project, consider how you will employ the structures of narrative, analysis, and argument to construct your reflective project. Draft an essay that begins with a brief narrative about your attitudes and abilities as you began the course and how those attitudes and abilities influenced the choices that you made as you began these writing projects, what you learned from completing the projects, what abilities and skills you will take with you from the course, and what you need to work on to improve your writing in the future.

   Narrative: In the reflective project, you might want to imagine the progress of this course as a sort of journey that you undertook that led you from your initial attitude and abilities to those you have now. In the reflective project, you will want to describe this journey for your ideal community of readers— for yourself, for your teacher, for your classmates, and for students who will be taking this course in the future.

Analysis: As with all narratives, it will be important to interrupt the story to apply analysis. Make sure that your reflective project also provides an analysis of why your attitudes and abilities changed, what assignments and knowledge led to that change, and exactly how the work you did improved your writing and revealed what you do well as a writer and what you need to improve. Try to trace these elements to specific projects and specific moments where you realized something about your writing that caused you to work to improve it.

Argument: In this essay, you are basically arguing that something or some things have changed about your attitudes and abilities as a writer and for the need to set some goals for further improvement. As such, the goal is to convince the reader that your knowledge, attitudes, and abilities as a writer have changed, and that certain assignments, knowledge, and work on specific projects caused those changes. Be as specific about these elements as you possibly can be.

3. **Peer Review**: After you complete the first draft, send it out for peer review. As your classmates have seen your writing throughout the course, they may be in a position to help you further define what changes have taken place in your writing.

4. **The Visual**: Look at the visual images you have selected for your projects and plan a short section in your reflective project on how this element of the course has affected your idea of how images can help the rhetoric of your projects. Select an appropriate visual image to accompany your reflective project.

5. **Revision and Proofing**: After you have selected your visual, completed your peer reviews, and received your peer-reviewed draft back, make revisions, and check your sentences. Check your work against the Checklist of Questions for Process (p. 27). As always, you will want to read your final draft aloud before you consider it complete. After you are confident of your revision and proofing, save your file. Follow the instructions for uploading the project.

Peer Review Questionnaire for the Reflective Project

Your Name:

Title of the essay you are peer reviewing:

Author of the essay:

Answer the following questions about the project you are reviewing in a complete sentence or in a short paragraph.

1. Summarize what main changes the writer sees in his own work. Are these the changes you have observed? If not, point out some other changes you have seen in this writer's work:

2. Describe what you have liked most about this writer's projects:

3. What was the most interesting thing you remember from reading this writer's projects?

4. Did you learn anything from reading this writer's work throughout the course that you applied to your own writing? What was that?

5. If the writer has included a visual image with the project, how do you think the visual adds to the project? Does it seem appropriate to the project? Does it contribute to the project? How? Could you suggest a more useful or appropriate visual for the project?

FINDING AND EVALUATING SOURCES

When you incorporate what others have said about an issue into your writing projects, you are using the words and ideas of those other authors to increase the credibility, the logic, and the emotional appeal of your own argument. The idea of incorporating others' works into your projects is not to let those other authors take over the essay you are writing, but to use those words and ideas to help you make your own arguments.

While the Internet has made it much easier to access information, the Internet also encourages some inexperienced researchers to simply rely on a few search engines such as Google, Yahoo or Bing to gather information. The problem with these search engines is that they can lead to the impression that research is simply a matter of "surfing the net."

When students do try to use search engines to research their topics, they often find that the amount of information is either overwhelming (plugging the word "environment" into Google produces almost two billion "hits") or seemingly non-existent (plugging the phrase "the problem of toxic waste in Rhode Island" produces zero "hits"). The problem is that searching for a term or a phrase that is not focused enough produces too many results, and searching for a term that is too focused will not produce any results.

A better strategy is to start by searching sources of information that have been designed specifically for serious researchers. These sources of information include the electronic catalogues of your local academic library, which will connect you to the library's own collection of research and to databases such as Academic Search Premier, FirstSearch, InfoTrac, JSTOR, LexisNexis, EBSCOHost, Project Muse, and others. Google also includes a more scholarly web search at google.scholar. com. These databases contain information that has been collected and evaluated as suitable for serious researchers.

EVALUATING SOURCES

When you do find material that you plan to use for your writing projects outside of these traditional sources, such as information you have found by searching through a search engine like Google or Yahoo, you must evaluate that source for yourself to determine whether the information is likely to be reliable or not. In order to evaluate the source, look for the following indicators:

❏ Authority. Try to establish who the "author" of the website is. Generally, serious sites will give a short statement on or link you to the author's credentials, but if that is not available, then you might try looking up other sources by the same author to establish his or her credibility.

❏ Objectivity. Try to establish what group or organization has sponsored the website. Sites that have an address that ends in .edu are sponsored by educational institutions such as universities and colleges, but individual students and teachers can often post information even to these sites that has not been evaluated. Sites whose addresses end in .org or .com or .gov are, of course, sponsored either by organizations, companies, or the government. If the web site uses a dot com extension, it is trying to sell you something. You may assume that organization and government sites are credible; however, even these sites need to be evaluated for unintentional or intentional bias. Is the information on the site fact or opinion?

❏ Accuracy. Check the quality of the website. Does it look professional with regard to the quality of design, images and writing? Is it free from spelling and grammatical errors? Make sure that the information on the site provides sources for any cited information. Any quotations, statistics, facts, or ideas that do not seem original to the author of the website should have some indication of where the website obtained that information.

❏ Currency. Check the date of the website's last update if it is provided (usually at the bottom of the site). Check the links on the site to make sure they are still active. If the links on the site do not work, then the website has probably not been updated for a while.

COMMON KNOWLEDGE, INCORRECT SOURCING, AND FRAUD

While some people may assume that students easily know what needs to be cited and what does not need to be cited, the truth is that sometimes making this judgment can be difficult. **Common knowledge** generally does not have to be documented; however, establishing just what common knowledge is can be difficult. Briefly, common knowledge includes information that just about anyone might know or that can be found in a variety of sources without reference. For instance, everyone basically "knows" the story of how American astronauts landed on the moon. If, for some reason, you wanted to make reference to that event in your essay, you might have to look up the exact date of the moon landing (July 20, 1969), the name of the Lunar Module (the Eagle) and the full name and/or last name of the astronaut that was the first to stand on the moon (Neil Armstrong). Even so, all that information would likely be considered common knowledge because it is readily available in a wide variety of sources. However, let us suppose that we wanted to make reference to the analysis of Jim Scotti, who is Senior Research Specialist at the University of Arizona's Lunar and Planetary Lab, that the moon landing could not have been faked because all the evidence that humans did go to the moon "fits together too well to be a fake." Then we would need to cite the source ("Non-Faked Moon Landings" http:// pirlwww.lpl.arizona.edu/~jscotti /NOT_faked/).

Likewise, it would not be necessary to provide a source for the commonly known fact that many people die as a direct result of smoking cigarettes every year, but if we were to write that smoking is directly or indirectly responsible for one in five deaths in the U.S. each year, then we would want to cite our source (Public Citizen. "Family Values, Killer Industries: Whose Family, What Values?" *Congress Watch*. 20 August 2006 <http://www.citizen.org/congress/campaign/archive/articles.cfm?ID=5421>).

PLAGIARISM

Students are often worried about the possibility of committing plagiarism, and the potential does exist for students to make mistakes in judging what needs to be cited and how to properly cite a source. There is never any reason for a student to commit unintentional plagiarism in a course, however. When in doubt, always ask your teacher. What follows are a few guidelines to help you.

Basically, plagiarism, is defined by *Webster's International Dictionary* as "to steal or purloin and pass off as one's own the ideas, words, or artistic production of another; to use without credit the ideas, expressions, or productions of another." For the sake of clarity, we use the word "fraud" instead of plagiarism for the *intentional* representation of someone else's ideas or words as your own. It is also important to realize that the unintentional use of others' words (as sometimes happens when you cut and paste information into your paper and then forget to acknowledge its source) is considered plagiarism. The rules are the rules, and student writers must follow them. In other words, not meaning to have copied someone else's words is not an acceptable excuse for plagiarism. Briefly, each paper that you turn in and every sentence in it must be written completely by you, or you must give proper credit to the other writers for their ideas and words. In addition, most teachers consider handing in papers that were written for other classes to be fraud or plagiarism. New papers should be written for each assignment unless your teacher indicates otherwise. Remember that writing teachers are experienced at picking out papers that contain plagiarism, so do not be tempted to download papers from the web or to "recycle" papers from other students. These things are also examples of plagiarism.

Most people consider plagiarism to be the ethical [OR the moral] equivalent to lying, cheating, and stealing. When you plagiarize, you have stolen another writer's hard work. Further, you have shortchanged your own education and compromised your ethics. Additionally, you risk damaging your grade for the assignment or the course, and you risk damaging your GPA and your academic or professional career. Plagiarism, specifically the kind we identify as fraud, is a very serious academic offense. In a way, the very foundation of the American educational system rests on the issue of trust, and this trust depends on an honest exchange between students and their teachers. Just as students need to trust that teachers are honest about grading, teaching, and advising, teachers need to trust that students will be honest when taking tests and writing papers. Intentional plagiarism, or any type of cheating, seriously undermines this foundation. This sort of dishonesty or carelessness also indicates that there may be serious questions about the offending student's ethics, and the stigma of this unethical behavior may follow the student for years, decreasing the student's chances of success in academic and professional work.

Turning in a paper that was written or partially written by anyone else is also considered fraud. Obviously, "anyone else" includes **everyone** but you. You should not turn in a paper that was written or partially written by a parent, a boyfriend or girlfriend, a spouse, sibling, friend, stranger, tutor or another student, a professional or amateur author, or anyone else.

There are other types of plagiarism that students may fall prey to, most notably "**patchwriting**" and incorrect or insufficient documentation. Patchwriting is taking several different texts that were written by others, piecing together those ideas or words into a single paper, and turning in that paper as your own work. Incorrect or insufficient documentation occurs when not enough of the original language and sentence structure of the source is changed for a paraphrase or when another author's words or ideas are used without giving the author proper credit. To paraphrase correctly, major words and basic sentence structure must be changed from the original. A paper should never be made up of a series of paraphrases of the work of others. Use paraphrasing only to support your own ideas and arguments and not to construct your paper. Occasionally, students do get confused about these two issues. If you are unsure about whether you have engaged in patchwriting or incorrect or insufficient documentation, you should talk to your teacher before you hand in your paper. If you are having trouble writing your paper, do not be tempted to plagiarize; instead, ask your teacher for additional help with the assignment.

You can get help writing your papers. All successful writers rely on other readers to help make their writing better. In fact, going to your university's writing center or having another student or friend read your papers before you turn them in is generally a good idea. Most classes will have peer review sessions that allow other students to read and comment on your papers. However, you should never let anyone else sit at the computer and type in words or hold the pen and write words on your paper. Ask peer reviewers and readers to limit their responses to letting you know where you might make changes (for example, word choice, having a clear point, confusing sentences, awkward structures, organization, spelling, etc.) Even if you decide to take a reader's advice, you should not let them make substantial changes to your work.

Good writers often research their topics to find sources to support their ideas, but if you write about what these other people have written on the subject or if you quote them, use their original ideas or language, or paraphrase their ideas, you must give them credit in your paper. All sources, no matter how briefly used, must be cited.

CITATION FORMATS

Writers have developed several different formats for signaling to readers that information comes from other sources. The two most common formats for including other author's work are MLA (Modern Language Association) style and APA (American Psychological Association) style. One of these two common formats is probably familiar to most experienced readers. Each is based on a very simple logic that signals to readers that they are reading an essay that makes reference to other sources. These formats tell your readers whether your essay is concerned with a topic from the Humanities or the Social Sciences. These formats also direct readers about how to find your sources, should they need or want to. Following are some basic instructions on how to incorporate quoted and paraphrased material into your writing; however, these are not all the possible types of sources you might run into when using another author's work; nor are they the only two styles in use. Consult your teacher, your writing center, or a complete guidebook from either MLA or APA for further information.

A Short Guide to Using Sources in MLA Style

Using Quotations Effectively in MLA Style

1. **Do not allow a quotation to stand alone. All quotations should be linked to a sentence or a phrase that you have written.**

Following is a "stand-alone" quotation:

> As our culture has grown more dependent on television as an escape from reality, we have become more isolated from our neighbors. "Americans used to be a great and restless people, fond of the outdoors in all of its manifestations" (Ehrenreich 79). I am not so sure that I agree with her completely, but she does, at least, point to part of the problem.

Note that the quoted sentence in the above paragraph has not been linked by an introductory clause or a set-up of any kind to a sentence or phrase that the writer of the essay has written. Link the quotation to your writing in one of these ways:

Link the quotation to a phrase:

> As our culture has grown more dependent on television as an escape from reality, we have become more isolated from our neighbors. Barbara Ehrenreich writes that "Americans used to be a great and restless people, fond of the outdoors in all of its manifestations" (79). I am not so sure that I agree with her completely, but she does, at least, point to part of the problem.

Link the quotation to a phrase with a comma:

> As our culture has grown more dependent on television as an escape from reality, we have become more isolated from our neighbors. As Barbara Ehrenreich writes, "Americans used to be a great and restless people, fond of the outdoors in all of its manifestations" (79). I am not so sure that I agree with her completely, but she does, at least, point to part of the problem.

Or,

> As our culture has grown more dependent on television as an escape from reality, we have become more isolated from our neighbors. "Americans used to be a great and restless people, fond of the outdoors in all of its manifestations" as Barbara Ehrenreich writes (79). I am not so sure that

I agree with her completely, but she does, at least, point to part of the problem.

Link the quotation to a complete sentence with a colon:

As our culture has grown more dependent on television as an escape from reality, we have become more isolated from our neighbors. Barbara Ehrenreich seems to agree: "Americans used to be a great and restless people, fond of the outdoors in all of its manifestations" (79). I am not so sure that I agree with her completely, but she does, at least, point to part of the problem.

2. **The first time you quote from an author, introduce or frame the quotation to provide a context for the borrowed passage.**

Unfortunately, America has now become a nation of lazy, overweight slobs. Barbara Ehrenreich, noted author and humorist, would seem to agree: "Americans used to be a great and restless people, fond of the outdoors in all of its manifestations" (79). Her opinion, which is contained in the essay "Spudding Out," is one that many people share.

Note that the quoted author has been introduced using her full name and has been identified as "noted author and humorist." Also notice that the title of the essay from which the quotation has been taken has been mentioned to give further context to the quotation.

After you have introduced an author by providing the appropriate context, you may then refer to the author by last name only when you quote him or her again.

3. **To put a quotation inside a quotation, use single quotes inside the double quotes.**

Barbara Ehrenreich provides some statistics: "In 1968, 85 percent of college students said that they hoped their education would help them 'develop a philosophy of life'" (81).

Note that in every case above, the author of the essay has attempted to give a context for the quotation and has also followed the quoted material with an original comment that is designed to explain the relationship of the quotation to the topic of the paragraph or a developing point. Never allow the quotation to just appear in the paper or allow the quotation to "have the last word." Always integrate the quotation into the point you are making by preparing the reader for the quotation before you insert it and by making a comment or explaining the quotation after it appears in your paper.

Also note that the punctuation goes inside the quote marks if there is no parenthetical citation and after the parenthetical citation if there is one.

4. **To introduce a quotation longer than four lines, use a colon and what is known as *block quotation* form. Indent 10 spaces, use no quote marks, then insert the parenthetical citation after skipping two spaces followed by a period outside the parenthesis.**

Ehrenreich notes that much has changed about the way students pick their majors and in their expectations for what life will be like after college:

> There has been a precipitous decline, just since the seventies, in the number of students majoring in mind-expanding but only incidentally remunerative fields like history and mathematics. Meanwhile, business—as an academic pursuit—is booming: almost one-fourth of all college graduates were business majors in 1983, compared to about one-seventh in 1973, while the proportions of those who major in philosophy or literature have vanished to less than 1 percent (79).

Notably, fewer college students are taking courses in humanities, while the demand for business courses has increased.

5. **Some other examples of appropriate use of quotations:**

A. **Single author named in the sentence:** After you have contextualized the author, you may refer to him or her by last name only. *Note the placement of the quote marks and the punctuation.*

Ehrenreich writes that "Americans used to be a great and restless people, fond of the outdoors in all of its manifestations" (79).

B. **Single author in the parenthetical:** If you do not include the author's name in the sentence, then you must include it in the parenthetical citation. *Note the placement of the quote marks and the punctuation.*

Now, we no longer spend as much time outdoors: "Americans used to be a great and restless people, fond of the outdoors in all of its manifestations" (Ehrenreich 79).

C. Two or more works by the same author: In this citation we are assuming that more than one essay by Barbara Ehrenreich will be cited. As such we should identify the title of the one we are citing here.

Ehrenreich writes that "Americans used to be a great and restless people, fond of the outdoors in all of its manifestations" ("Spudding Out" 79).

Now, we no longer spend as much time outdoors: "Americans used to be a great and restless people, fond of the outdoors in all of its manifestations" (Ehrenreich, "Spudding Out" 79).

D. Two or three authors: Just include both authors in either in-sentence citation or parenthetical citation.

According to Dobrin and Brown, "every indicator from the current market shows that a slowdown is inevitable" (350).

Some analysts believe that "every indicator from the current market shows that a slowdown is inevitable" (Dobrin and Brown 350).

E. More than three authors: For more than three authors, use the first author's name and the words et al., which is a Latin phrase meaning "and others."

The possibility is, of course, that "some countries will use the new law to circumvent current trade restrictions" (Olson et al. 256).

F. Authors with the same last name: If more than one of your sources has the same last name, then you must identify which author you are quoting by using the first name, too.

When carbon emissions reach a certain level, "a tipping point will have been reached where it will be too late to stop the major problems that are associated with global warming" (Richard Smith 25).

G. Organizational author: If the source has been "written" as an institutional document with no stated author, use the institutional name as you would the author.

The Rockridge Institute claims that "when a frame is applied to an issue, it leads people to think and reason about the issue in a specific way. Suddenly, certain conclusions seem to become inevitable and others become nearly impossible" (1).

Recent studies suggest that "when a frame is applied to an issue, it leads people to think and reason about the issue in a specific way. Suddenly, certain conclusions seem to become inevitable and others become nearly impossible" (Rockridge 1).

H. Website: Print sources and internet or electronic sources are formatted slightly differently in MLA Style. In print citations, there is no comma used between the author's last name and the page number. In electronic sources, there is a comma between the author's last name, and a paragraph number. Page numbers are no longer required for online sources. If the author is not identified then identify the website page by its title. Websites are not considered to have page numbers, so cite them as you would entire works.

I. Indirect source: When you use a quotation or a paraphrase that your source has cited from another source, use "qtd. in" (this means quoted in).

Dobrin notes that carbon emissions have reached "a dangerous tipping point" (qtd. in Drew 413).

J. Email or personal interview: Cite the name of the person whose email you are quoting or who you interviewed as you would an author.

Developing a Works Cited page in MLA Style

1. The works cited page begins on a new page.

2. The works cited page is entitled "Works Cited."

3. Each source you quote, paraphrase, or summarize in your paper must have a corresponding works cited entry.

4. Alphabetize the entries; do not number them.

5. Italicize titles of books, films, albums, and periodicals; put quotes around the titles of articles.

6. Capitalize all words in titles and subtitles except articles, prepositions, and infinitives.

7. Reduce publisher names by leaving off "and sons," "limited," "company," and "incorporated."

   Reduce University and Press to the abbreviation UP (no periods). Thus Oxford University Press becomes Oxford UP. State University of New York Press becomes SUNY P.

8. Do not use p. or pp. to indicate page numbers.

9. Use a hanging indent for all entries.

SAMPLE ENTRIES FOR A WORKS CITED PAGE IN MLA STYLE

A. A Book, Brochure, Pamphlet, or Graphic Novel, by a Single Author: Reprint the author's name exactly as they do and include the subtitle of the text. MLA also requires advising the reader the "medium" of the publication (Print, Web, Television, CD, Audiocassette, LP Audiotape, Digital Download, Film, Lecture, Speech Address, Reading, etc.)

> Hardin, Joe Marshall. *Opening Spaces: Critical Pedagogy and Resistance Theory in Composition.* Albany: SUNY P, 2001. Print.

B. A Book of Essays by Various Authors Edited by a Single Editor: Notice that the editor's name has been followed by the abbreviation "ed.," which has not been capitalized.

> Dobrin, Sidney I., ed. *Saving Place: An Ecocomposition Reader.* Boston: McGraw-Hill, 2005. Print.

C. A Book by Two Authors: Notice that the second author's name has not been reversed.

> Faigley, Lester, and Jack Selzer. *Good Reasons: Designing and Writing Effective Arguments.* NY: Longman, 2003. Print.

D. A Book of Essays by Various Authors Edited by Two Editors: Notice that the second editor's name has not been reversed.

> Weisser, Christian, and Sidney I. Dobrin, eds. *Ecocomposition: Theoretical and Pedagogical Approaches.* Albany: SUNY P, 2001. Print.

E. A Book by Three or More Authors: The Latin phrase "et al." means "and others."

> Sanchez, Julio, et al. *Things You Need to Know about Everything: What a Day*. Oxford: Oxford UP, 2005. Print.

F. Two or More Works by the Same Author: For the second entry by the same author use three dashes and a period. Alphabetize the entries by the first word of the title.

> Olson, Gary A. *Is There a Class in this Text?* London: Routledge, 2000. Print.

> ---. *Understanding Fish: Toward an Understanding of the Work of Stanley Fish*. Boston: Hide, 2002. Print.

G. Organizational Author: If the book or article has been "written" by an organization with no author cited, use the organization's name as if it were the author.

> Rockridge Institute. *What the Right Doesn't Want You to Know*. Sacramento: U of California P, 2001. Print.

H. Essay in an Edited Collection of Essays: The article by Julie Drew appears in the collection edited by Christian Weisser and Sidney I. Dobrin. Note the placement of the name of the collection and the editors' names.

> Drew, Julie. "The Politics of Place: Student Travelers and Pedagogical Maps." *Ecocomposition: Theoretical and Pedagogical Approaches*. Eds. Christian Weisser and Sidney I. Dobrin. Albany: SUNY P, 2001. Print.

I. Two or More Essays from the Same Collection: In this citation, two works (Drew and Bawarshi) have been cited from the same collection (Weisser and Dobrin). Entries must be made for all three works (Bawarshi, Drew, and Weisser and Dobrin). Retain the alphabetical order for each entry.

> Bawarshi, Anis. "The Ecology of Genre." Weisser and Dobrin 69-80. Print.

> Drew, Julie. "The Politics of Place: Student Travelers and Pedagogical Maps." Weisser and Dobrin 56-68. Print.

> Weisser, Christian, and Sidney I. Dobrin, eds. *Ecocomposition: Theoretical and Pedagogical Approaches*. Albany: SUNY P, 2001. Print.

J. Article in a Scholarly Journal: This citation is for the article by Giroux, which appears in the journal *JAC*. The volume number (20) and the issue number (1) have been included as has the year of the volume.

> Giroux, Henry A. "Public Pedagogy and Responsibility of Intellectuals: Youth, Littleton, and the Loss of Innocence." *JAC* 20 (2000): 9-44. Print.

K. Newspaper Article: Include the section number and the page on which the article begins (E1). The + is used to indicate that the article is continued on another page.

> Rodriquez, Pedro. "Students Find Outlet for Service Work through the Humane Society." *St. Petersburg Times* 4 Aug. 2001: E1+. Print.

L. Entire Website: This is the citation format for the opening (home) page of a particular website. The date given in the entry is the date the researcher first looked at the page. Note that MLA no longer requires the URL (the actual address).

> *The Rockridge Institute.* Web. 12 Apr. 2006.

M. Part of a Website: This is the citation format for a page that has been accessed from the homepage of the website above. This page has an author. Notice that the title of this page has been put in quotes, since it is like a "chapter" in a larger work. The larger work is the homepage.

> Lokoff, George. "Framing: It's About Values and Ideas." *The Rockridge Institute.* Web. 12 Apr. 2006.

N. Email or Personal Interview: For an email interview, just put "Email interview" instead of "Personal interview."

> Dobrin, Sidney I. Personal interview. 14 Apr. 2006.

A SHORT GUIDE TO USING SOURCES IN APA STYLE

In-text References

Generally speaking, to reference an author and a work in the text of an essay, cite the author and the year of publication of each in-text reference, connecting the two with a comma. For example: (Ehrenreich, 2001). Do not cite the page number unless you are directly quoting from the source.

If a work does not list an author, cite a shortened version of the title in the in-text citation, followed by a comma and the year of publication. For example, "America's Best," 2009). In-text citations are normally followed by a period outside of the information included in the in-text citation in parentheses.

For electronic sources, cite the title of the web page followed by a comma and the date, the same as for print sources. For conventions in citing direct quotations, see below.

Using Quotations Effectively in APA Style

1. **Never allow a quotation to stand alone. All quotations should be linked to a sentence or a phrase that you have written.**

Following is a "stand-alone" quotation:

> As our culture has grown more dependent on television as an escape from reality, we have become more isolated from our neighbors. "Americans used to be a great and restless people, fond of the outdoors in all of its manifestations" (Ehrenreich, 2001, p. 79). I am not so sure that I agree with her completely, but she does, at least, point to part of the problem.

Note that the quoted sentence has not been linked by a sentence or phrase that the writer of the essay has written. Link or connect the quotation with an introductory clause like this:

Link the quotation to a phrase:

> As our culture has grown more dependent on television as an escape from reality, we have become more isolated from our neighbors. Barbara Ehrenreich (2001) writes that "Americans used to be a great and restless people, fond of the outdoors in all of its manifestations" (p. 79). I am not so sure that I agree with her completely, but she does, at least, point to part of the problem.

Link the quotation to a short phrase with a comma:

> As our culture has grown more dependent on television as an escape from reality, we have become more isolated from our neighbors. As Barbara Ehrenreich (2001) writes, "Americans used to be a great and restless people, fond of the outdoors in all of its manifestations" (p. 79). I am not so sure that I agree with her completely, but she does, at least, point to part of the problem.

Or,

> As our culture has grown more dependent on television as an escape from reality, we have become more isolated from our neighbors. "Americans used to be a great and restless people, fond of the outdoors in all of its manifestations" as Barbara Ehrenreich (2001) writes (p. 79). I am not so sure that I agree with her completely, but she does, at least, point to part of the problem.

Link the quotation to a complete sentence with a colon:

> As our culture has grown more dependent on television as an escape from reality, we have become more isolated from our neighbors. Barbara Ehrenreich (2001) seems to agree: "Americans used to be a great and restless people, fond of the outdoors in all of its manifestations" (p. 79). I am not so sure that I agree with her completely, but she does, at least, point to part of the problem.

2. **The first time you quote from an author, introduce or frame the quotation to provide a context for the borrowed passage.**

> Unfortunately, America has now become a nation of lazy, overweight slobs. Barbara Ehrenreich (2001), noted author and humorist, would seem to agree: "Americans used to be a great and restless people, fond of the outdoors in all of its manifestations" (p. 79). Her opinion, which is contained in the essay "Spudding Out," is one that many people share.

Note that the quoted author has been introduced using her full name and has been identified as "noted author and humorist." Also notice that the title of the essay from which the quotation has been taken has been mentioned to give further context to the quotation.

After you have introduced an author by providing the appropriate context, you may then refer to the author by last name only when you quote him or her again.

3. **To put a quotation inside a quotation, use single quotes inside the double quotes:**

> Barbara Ehrenreich (2001) provides some statistics: "In 1968, 85 percent of college students said that they hoped their education would help them 'develop a philosophy of life'" (p. 81).

Note that in every case above, the author of the essay has given a context for the quotation and has also followed the quoted material with an original comment. Never allow the quotation to just appear in the paper or allow the quotation to "have the last word." Always integrate the quotation into the point you are making by preparing the reader for the quotation before you insert it and by making a comment or explaining the quotation after it appears in your paper.

Also note that the punctuation goes inside the quote marks if there is no parenthetical citation and after the parenthetical citation if there is one.

4. **To introduce a quotation longer than four lines, use a colon. When using quotations longer than 40 words, place them in a free-standing block that is indented five spaces from the left margin. Do not use quotation marks. The parenthetical citation comes after the closing punctuation mark. Note that the required comment following the quotation is not indented and is designed to place the quotation in context.**

Barbara Ehrenreich (2001) notes that much has changed about the way students pick their majors and in their expectations for what life will be like after college:

There has been a precipitous decline, just since the seventies, in the number of students majoring in mind-expanding but only incidentally remunerative fields like history and mathematics. Meanwhile, business—as an academic pursuit—is booming: almost one-fourth of all college graduates were business majors in 1983, compared to about one-seventh in 1973, while the proportions of those who major in philosophy or literature have vanished to less than 1 percent. (p. 79)

Notably, fewer college students are taking courses in humanities, while the demand for business courses has increased.

5. **Some other examples of appropriate use of quotations:**

As our culture has grown more dependent on television as an escape from reality, we have become more isolated from our neighbors. As Barbara Ehrenreich (2001) writes in an essay entitled "Spudding Out," which first appeared in her book *The Worst Years of Our Lives*, "Americans used to be a great and restless people, fond of the outdoors in all of its manifestations" (p. 79). Now, she writes, we use television to hide from the world. If she is right then this is surely a tragedy.

   As our culture has grown more dependent on television as an escape
   from reality, we have become more isolated from our neighbors.
   Barbara Ehrenreich (2001) writes that "Americans used to be a great
   and restless people, fond of the outdoors in all of its manifestations"
   ("Spudding Out," p. 79). Now, she continues, television may be "the only
   place to hide" (p. 82). If she is right then this is surely a tragedy.

6. Website: Websites are treated in the text much the same as print sources.
If possible, use the same author-date in-text citation style. If the author is not
identified then identify the website page by its title. Websites are not considered
to have page numbers, so cite them as if you would entire works. When provided,
identify online sources that you quote directly by paragraph number. Use "para." or
the figure denoting paragraph. If paragraphs are not numbered but the document
includes headings, provide the heading title and identify the paragraph number
under that heading.

7. Indirect source: When you use a quotation or a paraphrase that your source
has cited from another source, use "as quoted in," followed by the author of the
source you are quoting.

   Dobrin notes that carbon emissions have reached "a dangerous tipping point"
   (as quoted in Drew, 2004).

8. Email or personal interview: To quote from informal conversations,
whether personal, over the phone, or by email, cite the name of the person who you
are referring to in the sentence and include the type of communication and the date
of the communication in the parentheses.

   Dobrin (personal communication, April 12, 2006) believes that carbon
   emissions have reached a point where there may be no turning back the ill
   effects of global warming.

Paraphrasing in APA Style

If you are summarizing or paraphrasing materials from a source, you need only add
the usual author-date in-text citation. It should follow directly after the portion of
the text that you have summarized:

   Some scientists agree that carbon emissions have now reached a critical phase.
   (Drew, 2004).

Developing a Reference page in APA style.

1. The reference page begins on a new page.

2. Center the title of the page, and call it References.

3. Each source you quote, paraphrase or summarize in your paper must have a corresponding works cited entry, excepting personal communications of any kind, including email communications. In these cases, the in-text citation is considered sufficient.

4. List authors last name first followed by the first or both initials for each author. If there is more than one author, list each author's name last name first, followed by their initials.

5. Alphabetize all entries including both authors and title names (do not alphabetize using "the" or "a").

6. Italicize titles of books and periodicals; do not put quotes around the titles of articles. Underlining is no longer acceptable.

7. Capitalize only the first word of the titles and the first word of the subtitles.

8. Use a .5 hanging indent for all entries. This can be formatted under the "paragraph" function in MS Word by selecting the "Hanging Indent" option in the drop-down menu options for First Line.

Sample Entries for a Reference Page in APA Style

A. Book by a single author:

Hardin, J. M. (2001). *Opening spaces: Critical pedagogy and resistance theory in composition.* Albany: State University of New York Press.

B. Book of essays by various authors edited by a single editor:

Dobrin, S. I. (Ed.). (2005). *Saving place: an ecocomposition reader.* Boston, MA: McGraw-Hill.

C. Book by two authors:

Faigley, L., Selzer, J. (2003). *Good reasons: Designing and writing effective arguments.* New York: Longman.

D. Book of essays by various authors edited by more than one editor:

Weisser, C., Dobrin, S. I. (Eds). (2001). *Ecocomposition: Theoretical and pedagogical approaches.* Albany, NY: State Univ. of New York Press.

E. Book by six or more authors:

Sanchez, R., Hardin, J. M., Drew, J., Dobrin, S. I., Brown, S. G., Greenbaum, A., . . . Olson, G. A. (2005). *Things you need to know about everything: What a day.* Oxford, England: Oxford University Press.

F. Two or more works by the same author:

Olson, G. A. (2002). *Understanding Fish: Toward an understanding of the work of Stanley Fish.* Boston, MA: Hide Press.

Olson, G. A. (2000). *Is there a class in this text?* London, England: Routledge Publications.

G. Organizational author:

Rockridge Institute. (2001). *What the right doesn't want you to know.* Sacramento, CA: University of California Press: Author.

H. Essay in a collection of essays:

Drew, J. (2001). The politics of place: Student travelers and pedagogical maps. In C. Weisser and S. I. Dobrin (Eds.), *Ecocomposition: Theoretical and pedagogical approaches* (pp. 62-72). Albany, NY: State University of New York Press.

I. Article in a scholarly journal (with and without assigned DOI):

Giroux, H. A. (2000). Public pedagogy and responsibility of intellectuals: Youth, Littleton, and the loss of innocence. *JAC, 20,* 9.

Article in a scholarly journal with DOI assigned:

Waters, A. (2007). Native-speakerism in ELT: Plus ca change? System, 35(3), 281-292. doi:10.1016/j.system.01.002 [Available online 13 August 2007].

J. Magazine article without DOI assigned, found in library database:

Hubbard, L. (2009, May 11). Surging demand for defunct energy drink. Convenience Store News, 45(6), 16. Retrieved August 4, 2009, from EBSCO MegaFILE database.\

[THIS CITATION IS QUOTED FROM THE UMC Library Online APA References crib sheet]

K. Newspaper article

Rodriquez, P. (2001, August 8). Students find outlet for service work through the Humane Society. St. Petersburg Times, p. E1.

L. Entire website:

Note that online reference works should identify the kind of file, which is to be followed by "Retrieved from" and the full online URL.

The Rockridge Institute. (2004). Retrieved from http://www. rockridgeinstitute.org.

L. Part of a website:

Lakoff, G. (2006). Framing: It's about values and ideas. In *The Rockridge Institute*. Retrieved April 12, 2006, from http://www. rockridgeinstitute.org/research/lakoff/valuesideas.

NEW TO APA: the DOI

A DOI is a "digital object identifier," a unique string of numbers and letters that are assigned to authors who apply for them by a registration agency called the International DOI Foundation. The publisher will assign a DOI when an author's article is published and becomes available electronically.

All DOI numbers begin with the numerals 10 and contain a prefix and a suffix separated by a slash. APA recommends that, when DOIs are available, you include them in your References list for both print and electronic sources. You can locate the DOI on the first page of the electronic journal article, near the copyright notice, or on the database landing page of the article.

In the back of many writing textbooks you often find lists of rules about grammar, which are generally stated in terms of something you must or must not do. Whatever the grammar rule is, it is generally followed by a few examples of the rule being violated and then corrected. Sometimes, the textbook will then present a few exercises, and you are required to decide which sentences are correct and which are incorrect and instructed to correct the "wrong" ones. The theory of this type of instruction is that once you have read the rule and practiced the exercises that you will be able to avoid making that particular mistake in your own writing. This type of instruction may work for people who are highly motivated to learn this way, but research generally suggests that not many students show significant improvement in their writing after this type of instruction. In fact, students generally find this process particularly unsatisfactory and mostly mysterious.

In my own classes, I often asked students where they think these grammar rules come from. In almost every class, students will suggest that English teachers have developed these grammar rules, but these grammar rules are more correctly understood as a changing description of how people use language in their daily communications. The rules are not so much "invented" by English teachers as they are created by actual writers.

GRAMMAR OR USAGE?

Actually, the word "grammar" is not the correct term to describe the problems that writers have with their sentences and word choices. "Grammar" is best understood as a term from the field of linguistics that describes the way any language uses its words to construct sentences. What we are really talking about in this section is more correctly called **usage conventions**. The word "convention," which has appeared in several places in this book, describes the way writers generally do things. So "usage conventions" describes the way words are most frequently used in the English language and the way sentences are generally put together by actual writers. The idea, in most cases, is that writers make conscious choices about what words to use and how to construct their sentences, and they generally choose words and structures that will make their writing understandable to the greatest number of readers. Over time, these choices become conventional. Using appropriate conventions of sentence structure and word choice contributes to the writer's credibility, as well. True, experienced writers sometimes find places in their writing where sentences seem to work better if the accepted usage conventions are violated on purpose, but as with all rhetorical choices, writers need to think about what readers will expect of particular genres and particular types of writing. Once again, it is about the choices you make. All effective, serious writers have reference books for style and usage and do not hesitate to look up answers to questions they have about sentence structures and word choices. Following are some of the major usage issues that writers generally have.

WORDS I—SPELL-CHECKERS, MISUSED WORDS, POSSESSION AND CONTRACTION

Spell-checkers: The very least you should do for your readers is to run your word processor's spell-checker over your writing before you consider having someone else read it. The spell-checker is only the first step, of course, but most readers these days will consider misspelled words to be almost insulting, since almost everyone has a word processor with a spell-checker. Still, the word processor does not know whether you mean "there," "their," or "they're," so reading your work carefully and having someone else read it before you consider it complete is vital.

Misused Words: The difference between "there," "their," and "they're" is more than just a spelling problem. These words all mean something different, and we sometimes use the wrong one because they sound alike. The most common of these misused words are:

a and an: "a" is used before a consonant sound, and "an" is used before a vowel sound: *a lamp, a book, a history lesson, an opera, an onion, an igloo.*

accept and except: "accept" means to receive something; "except" means "to exclude" something: *I will accept all of your argument except the second point.*

advice and advise: "advice" is the noun and "advise" is the verb: *I advise you to listen to this advice.*

affect and effect: "affect" is usually the verb, which means "to influence"; "effect" is usually the noun, which means the "result": *Being consciously aware of some usage conventions will affect your grade. The effect of consciously choosing usage conventions is better writing.*

can and may: "may" is generally used to mean "permission"; "can" indicates ability": *You may attend the concert if you can find tickets.*

cite and site: "site" is a particular place; "cite" is to quote or reference something: *You may use a quotation from a good site on the web, as long as you cite your source.*

complement and compliment: "complement" means "to go with" or "to complete"; "compliment" means "to flatter": *Let me compliment you on your complementary wardrobe.*

farther and further: if you mean to indicate actual distance, use "farther"; if you mean quantity or degree, use "further": *Farther up the road, we will stop and discuss this further.*

its and it's: "it's" is always a contraction meaning "it is"; "its" is the possessive of "it": *It's imperative that we discuss this problem and its implications.*

lie and lay: "lie" generally means "to recline" or "to rest on a surface"; "lay" means "to put or place something": *Lay your backpack on the counter and lie down on the couch.*

loose and lose: "loose" is the opposite of "tight"; "lose" is the acting of misplacing something: *If your rope is loose, then you may lose your footing.*

past and passed: these two words have very different meanings: *The "past" always refers to time that has "passed."*

set and sit: you "sit" down, or something will "sit" on the counter if you "set" it there: *Set your books on the counter and sit down on the couch.*

since and sense: these words are often confused, but they are not interchangeable: *Since you obviously have no sense of direction; I will look at a map.*

then and than: "then" is always about time; "than" is about comparisons: *I then decided that he was more intelligent than I.*

there, their, and they're: "there" is always about place, or it can be used in sentences like "there are only two books on the table"; "their" is always possessive; "they're" is always the contraction of "they are": *They're putting their books over there.*

to, too, and two: "two" is, of course, the number; "too" indicates a quantity, as in "too much" or "too few"; or, it may also be used in place of the word "also"; almost every other usage is "to": *In order not to have too many choices; I, too, will limit my selection to two books.*

toward and towards: these words are basically interchangeable, but in American English, we generally use "toward" instead of "towards."

where and were: "where" is always about place; "were" is the verb: *Where were you going?*

whether, weather, and rather: "weather" refers to the temperature, precipitation, and such; "whether" refers to a choice, and is sometimes confused with "rather": *Whether you choose to attend or not; I would rather not go if the weather is bad.*

your and you're: "your" is the possessive pronoun; "you're" is always the contraction for "you are": *You're going to need your raincoat.*

Contractions: Many students have been told never to use contractions in academic papers. However, there may be some cases where the situation for the writing calls for a more "relaxed" tone, in which contractions may be acceptable. Like all choices in writing, the decision of whether to use contractions or not should be made according to the situation, the genre, and the ideal community of readers for the specific piece of writing. Most readers and writers will have little problem with "don't," "isn't," "wouldn't," "couldn't" and other typical contractions, but be very careful when using contractions that substitute for subject/verb constructions such as "I'm," "they're," and "you're," which stand in for "I am," "they are," and "you are." Even experienced writers will sometimes accidentally use "their" when they mean "they're" and "your" when they mean "you're." It is so easy to make this error that many writers just avoid contractions altogether.

Remember that "can't" is the contraction for "cannot" and that "cannot" is generally one word. There are exceptions, of course, and at times, writers will emphasize the "not" by making "cannot" into two words: "can not." Generally, though, "cannot" is one word.

Possession: In English, the possessive form of a noun is generally formed by adding an apostrophe and an "s" or by simply adding the apostrophe. Think of it this way: the apostrophe is really another kind of contraction, used to stand in for the word "his":

Bill his hat.

Bill's hat.

So the apostrophe can be thought of as really another form of contraction, in which the word "his" has been left out. This goes for feminine nouns or nouns that have no gender, as well.

Susie his artwork

The company his profits.

Susie's artwork.

The company's profits.

Inexperienced writers often get confused because they see some words that have only the apostrophe without the added "s" to make them plural. The convention is that if the word is a longer word that ends in "s" that you want to make possessive, then you may add the apostrophe and leave off the extra "s."

Socrates' argument.

The Jones' house.

There are no absolute rules for what constitutes a long word, though. The writer has the choice of adding the extra "s" or leaving it off.

Apostrophes are almost never used to make words plural. The exceptions are with numbers and letters:

I am not old enough to remember the 1950's.

There were seven A's in the class.

There are a few words that even experienced writers sometimes misuse when making plurals and possessives. Be very careful that you know the difference between these spellings:

| company | company's | companies | companies' |
| society | society's | societies | societies' |

Most spelling, contraction, and possession issues can be resolved by careful reading of the work. Experienced writers get used to mentally checking for commonly misspelled and misused words as they proofread their own or another's writing. Once again, reading your work out loud and having others read it as forms of proofreading are your best defense against these kinds of common mistakes.

Words II—Global and Gender-neutral Language

Global Issues: These days, readers are likely to have varied backgrounds that may hinder their understanding of cultural references and common clichés. In addition, many businesses and professions operate across national and cultural lines, so writers must learn to be careful about including words, phrases, and expressions for which readers with other cultural backgrounds will have no understanding. For instance, American writers will sometimes use phrases such as "in the ballpark," "bottom line," or "at the end of the day." These clichés are generally culturally specific to American English, and readers with other cultural backgrounds may take them literally.

Gender-neutral Language: The use of "gender-neutral" language is just a good choice. It is not a "communist plot," "political correctness," or a scam perpetrated by "feminazis." It is just good rhetoric. Plus, it is probably required for writing produced for most companies and in most professions; it is required in all documents used and approved by local, state, and federal agencies. Very few rational people advocate extremes, such as in turning "manhole cover" and "history" into "personhole cover" or "herstory." Using gender-neutral language is merely a way to include more readers and reflects the realities of our modern world:

Avoid	Use
Mrs.	Ms
manpower	human resources, work force
mankind	humankind, people
modern man	modern society, modern civilization
chairman	chairperson, chair, presiding officer
congressman	member of Congress, representative
fireman	firefighter
stewardess	flight attendant
policeman	police officer
salesman	sales agent
founding fathers	pioneers, founders
gentleman's agreement	informal agreement, oral contract

each nurse treats her patient with care	each nurse treats patients with care
a president sets his own agenda	presidents set their own agendas
every employee should sign his own card	all employees should sign their own cards

While the use of "his or hers," "him or her," "he or she," "him- or herself," etc. is awkward, it is correct unless you know for sure the gender of your reader. Changing pronouns to the plural is often the best way to fix this problem: "Each student must complete his or her own work" becomes "all students must complete their own work." Make sure that your pronouns (his, her, them, their) agree in number with their referents.

There is no reason to use odd constructions like he/she, him/her, or s/he. The English language is perfectly equipped for this: just use "he or she" or "him or her."

Word III—Vague Words and Clichés

Vague Words: There are no words that are absolutely forbidden under the right circumstances, and that includes what are normally called "vague" words. Still, you should keep an eye out for vague words and phrases as you are proofreading your work and that of others. Basically, these vague words come in three main types: vague nouns, vague verbs, and vague quantifiers.

1. **Vague nouns**: One of the jobs of a skilled writer is to make it clear in each sentence exactly what it is that he or she is writing about. Often, inexperienced writers will introduce vague nouns into their writing, which makes it hard for the reader to keep up with what the subject of the sentence is:

   There are three aspects of the advertisement that deal with the myth of cowboys. This is talked about in many ways by critics.

In the first place, both of these sentences above are "expletive" or "dummy subject" sentences. In other words, the things that are being written about in the sentence are not named as the actual subjects of the sentences. Instead, the subject of the first sentence is "there" and the subject in the second sentence is "these." You can make these sentences stronger by moving the "actor" of the sentences into the subject position:

   Three aspects of the advertisement deal with the myth of cowboys. Critics talk about these aspects in many ways.

Any time you begin a sentence with "there are," "it is," or similar "expletive" constructions, you might consider rewording those sentences.

Secondly, you might consider replacing the noun "aspects," since you might think of a more specific word to describe the "aspects" of an advertisement. What kind of "aspects" are they? Are they "design elements," "symbols," "images?"

> *Three design elements of the advertisement deal with the myth of cowboys.*
> *Critics talk about these elements in many ways.*

By removing the vague nouns, we have begun to improve these sentences. Do not be afraid of repeating yourself too much by using the specific nouns for the things you are writing about. Experienced writers work hard to find different words to vary their sentences without resorting to the use of vague nouns.

2. **Vague verbs**: Another cause of weak sentences is weak verbs. Having strong, specific, active verbs is vital to writing exciting sentences:

> *Three design elements of the advertisement deal with the myth of cowboys.*
> *Critics talk about these elements in many ways.*

Let us first replace "deal with" with a more specific verb. How do the design elements "deal with" the myth of cowboys? Do they "suggest" the myth of cowboys? Do they "promote" the myth? Do they "relate to" the myth?

> *Three design elements of the advertisement relate to the myth of cowboys.*
> *Critics talk about these elements in many ways.*

That makes the first sentence stronger but what could we do to strengthen the second? First, it is generally conventional to discuss what others have written about a subject by avoiding words like "talks" and "says" and using words like "discuss," "analyze," "argue," and other more specific verbs:

> *Three design elements of the advertisement relate to the myth of cowboys.*
> *Critics discuss these elements in many ways.*

Using stronger, more specific verbs will almost always improve your sentences.

3. **Vague Quantifiers**: Vague quantifiers may also weaken sentences:

> *Three design elements of the advertisement relate to the myth of cowboys.*
> *Critics discuss these elements in many ways.*

One place we could still strengthen our sentences is at the very end of the second sentence. We should be explaining to the reader just how critics discuss the design elements. The sentence does suggest that the writer will then explain how "critics discuss these elements." However, it would probably be better to go ahead and indicate this:

Three design elements of the advertisement relate to the myth of cowboys.
Critics discuss these elements in at least four ways.

There is no absolute set of rules about what words should never be used in your writing, of course. As with almost every other choice you can make about your writing, the situation—including the genre, the topic, and the ideal community of readers—must dictate the appropriateness of the language. Still, if you begin to work on getting vague words out of your writing as you revise and proofread, you will be taking the first steps toward stronger, more effective writing.

Clichés: Sometimes, writers will employ clichés. The reason that some phrases become clichés is, of course, because everyone uses them, and so effective writers will often work to eliminate as many clichés from their work as possible in order to strengthen their own credibility. Readers will want to read your ideas, opinions, and arguments in your own language and not hear the same old clichés. In addition, many clichés are culturally specific and will not translate well to readers from other cultures. As you look at this partial list of clichés and suggested replacements, ask yourself how each might be misunderstood by a reader from another culture:

Cliché	Possible Replacement
the bottom line	final cost, ultimate expense
at the end of the day	finally
in the ballpark	approximately
up the creek	in trouble
water under the bridge	forgiven
face the music	accept the consequences
pass the buck	deny accountability
worth its weight in gold	very valuable
sink or swim	succeed or fail

rise to the occasion	perform as expected
give 110 percent	over-achieve
hit the nail on the head	exactly right
in today's ever-changing society	in the last 10 years of American culture
due to the fact that	because

The above list is not complete, of course, as it would take many pages to consider every cliché and its possible replacement. The trick is to read your work carefully with the goal of making your writing as direct, as clear, and as unique as possible.

PUNCTUATION—PERIODS, COLONS, SEMI-COLONS, AND COMMAS

Some of the most misunderstood usage conventions are the ones about punctuation marks. Generally, we all know how to use periods at the end of sentences, but the use of colons, semi-colons, and commas is often more difficult to understand clearly. Actually, if you think about what the punctuation does in the sentence, it then becomes easier to use. Punctuation marks simply signal how readers should read and understand a particular sentence, and every change in punctuation will cause something different to happen in readers' minds as they read. Skilled writers have learned to place their punctuation marks with an awareness of how they work.

1. The **period (.)**: Most of us realize that periods come at the end of sentences to signal that a sentence—a complete idea—has been completed. As written English evolved, it became conventional to put a small dot, a period, at the end of a complete idea and to start the next idea with a larger, capitalized, letter. But what does it mean to say that a sentence is a complete idea?

In order to have a complete idea, you must be thinking about something (the **subject**) and you must think that some action is happening to that subject (the **predicate**, which contains the **verb**), even if that action is simply that the thing you are thinking about exists:

I am.

"I am" is a complete sentence—a complete idea—because there is something being thought about ("I") and something is happening to it ("am"). Increasing the number of subjects and the number of things happening to those subjects does not change the convention:

> *Bill, his friends, and several of the people from the office go to the park every weekend and play football.*

Each complete idea—each sentence—needs to have a subject and a predicate. If not, you have a **fragment**. If you have trouble with writing fragments, the best thing to do is simply to read your sentences out loud and to listen carefully to hear if the sentence includes something that you are thinking about and that something is happening to that thing.

2. The **colon (:)**: The colon is actually fairly simple to use, although many people have a wrong idea of what it really does. Briefly, a colon introduces any type of material that comes at the end of a sentence. You can introduce a single word:

> *There is one reason to buy our product: reliability.*

You can introduce a phrase:

> *There is one reason to buy our product: excellent reliability.*

You can introduce another sentence:

> *There is one reason to buy our product: it is reliable.*

Or you can introduce a list of items:

> *There are three reasons to buy our product: reliability, ease of repair, and cost.*

Most people believe that colons always precede lists, but as you can see, a colon may be used to introduce just about anything. The way to check that you have used the colon correctly is to substitute the word "namely" where you are thinking about using the colon:

> *There is one reason to buy our product (namely) reliability.*

> *There is one reason to buy our product (namely) excellent reliability.*

> *There is one reason to buy our product (namely) it is reliable.*

There are three reasons to buy our product (namely) reliability, ease of repair, and cost.

The "namely" test is not infallible, but it will generally give you an idea of where you might include a colon.

There are two small things to watch out for when using a colon. The first is that you generally do not see the colon following a verb:

Bill's friends are: Ziggy, Tom, and Vivian.

The reason is that the action of the verb introduces the items that follow it. The second thing to watch for is that you already have some word or phrase that does the introducing:

There are three reasons to buy our product, for example: reliability, ease of repair, and cost.

If you read that sentence and substitute the word "namely" for the colon, then you have both a phrase ("for example") and a piece of punctuation (:) doing that job:

There are three reasons to buy our product, for example, (namely): reliability, ease of repair, and cost.

Other words and phrases that generally do the same work as a colon are "such as," "for instance," and "including." You will generally not find a colon next to these words.

The fact is that conventional use of the colon is generally considered a high-level English skill. That seems surprising considering that, with just a little work and practice, almost anyone can learn how to use a colon. As we noted, many people believe that colons only come before lists. Colons may, however, introduce a word, a phrase, another sentence, or a list. Just check whether the word "namely" can be substituted. We suggest that you practice writing some sentences that include a colon and then watch for a chance to try them out in your own writing.

3. The **semi-colon (;)**: The semi-colon is designed to do two things: it joins two sentences, and it acts as a sort of "supercomma." Let us look at an example of how the semi-colon can be used to connect two sentences:

Bill is a good student. He studies all the time.

If we were to write an entire paragraph with this same type of sentence, it might become boring or distracting. Since these two sentences have a cause and effect relationship (Bill is a good student because he studies all the time), we can join them with a semi-colon.

Bill is a good student; he studies all the time.

Generally, the semi-colon can be used to connect any two sentences but is used most effectively when the two sentences have a cause and effect relationship of some sort or when they indicate opposites:

Bill is a good student; John is not.

Generally, it is considered acceptable to join two sentences together with a semi-colon if those sentences have a cause and effect relationship, are opposites, or when one makes a "comment" of some sort on the other. It is very important that you have a complete sentence on both sides of the semi-colon.

You may remember seeing a semi-colon used with words like "in fact," "however," "indeed," etc. This is basically the same thing as joining two sentences together; however, one of these words (they are called "conjunctive adjectives") is placed after the colon to clarify for the reader just what the relationship between the two sentences is:

Bill is a good student; however, he rarely studies.

The use of these conjunctive adjectives with the semi-colon is always structured the same way: the semi-colon, then the conjunctive adjective, and then the comma. Be careful that there is a sentence on both sides of the semi-colon, especially if you use one of these words. The same group of words can also have other uses:

Bill, however, is a good student.

In this case, "however" is merely an "interrupter" and needs to be surrounded by commas. So you must check to establish that you have a complete sentence on both sides of the semi-colon, whether you include the conjunctive adjective or not.

The semi-colon really only has one other conventional use. You may, if you have a large list of items that need to be sub-divided, use a semi-colon to sub-divide them:

I have lived in San Francisco, California, Natchitoches, Louisiana, Tampa, Florida, and Dallas, Texas.

This sentence is confusing because we need to indicate that the list of places needs to be sub-divided. We may use a semi-colon for that job:

I have lived in San Francisco, California; Natchitoches, Louisiana; Tampa, Florida; and Dallas, Texas.

When you need to, you may use the semi-colon as a sort of "supercomma."

As with learning other conventional uses of punctuation, there may be exceptions to these two conventional uses of the semi-colon. Nevertheless, if you practice using the semi-colon as outlined above, you will achieve some greater variation in your sentence structures.

4. The **comma (,)**: Although commas can seem confusing, they really only perform three functions: they separate more than two items in a list, they join two sentences together (with some help from a coordinating conjunction), and they attach non-essential, non-sentence information to sentences. Let us take a look at those uses one at a time:

A. First, you may use a comma to separate more than two items in a list:

I got up this morning, went downstairs, and drank a cup of coffee.

I will attend the meeting, finish writing this report, and meet you at the coffee shop.

The lists of things in the above two sentences has conveniently been marked by separating the three items with commas. This really just makes it easy for the reader to tell where one item leaves off and the other begins. Recently, it has become somewhat conventional to leave off the last comma:

I got up this morning, went downstairs and drank a cup of coffee.

I will attend the meeting, finish writing this report and meet you at the coffee shop.

Leaving the last comma off is actually more conventional in the field of journalism than anywhere else, though, and some have said that this got started as a way to save space in the newspaper (those commas add up, I guess). Generally, it is probably better to include the comma before the last item unless you are writing for a newspaper.

B. Along with the semi-colon, **a comma may also be used to join two sentences together, but only if the comma has the help of a coordinating conjunction** (for, and, nor, but, or, yet, so). The important thing to remember when you join two sentences together with a comma is that the comma must also be accompanied by a coordinating conjunction:

Bill is a good student, but he rarely studies.

The reason we can join the two sentences together with a comma and a coordinating conjunction is that the coordinating conjunction makes it clear what the relationship is between the two sentences. Without the coordinating conjunction, the comma does not supply the relationship between the two sentences and is not sufficient to hold them together.

Bill is a good student, he rarely studies.

You may already know that joining two sentences together with only a comma is known as a **comma splice**. The comma has been used to "splice," or join, the two sentences together. Look at this example carefully, as it is considered to be unconventional in most cases to splice two sentences together with only a comma. You may join two sentences together with a comma, but generally not without including a coordinating conjunction (for, and, nor, but, or, yet, so) to describe the relationship between the two sentences. Notice how the relationship between the two sentences changes if we use different coordinating conjunctions:

Bill is a good student, and he studies all the time.

Bill is a good student, so he studies all the time.

Bill is a good student, but he studies all the time.

Bill is a good student, for he studies all the time.

Readers may not be confused if you leave off the comma in this situation and just link the sentences with the coordinating conjunction, but it is generally best to use both. We suggest that you pay more attention to this type of comma use as you write in order to make it a more conscious choice. We also suggest that you try using various coordinating conjunctions to join sentences. "For," "nor," and "yet" are just as effective as "but," "so," "or," and "and."

Just to clarify, we should also note that joining two sentences together without any punctuation or linking word is considered unconventional:

Bill is a good student he studies all the time.

This sentence construction, in which two sentences have been joined without any punctuation or relationship words is known as a **run-on**. We prefer the term **fused**

sentences, though, as the term "run-on" tends to make people think that a sentence is simply too long. A run-on, or fused sentences, is simply two sentences that have been stuck together without any punctuation or words to explain their relationship.

So let us review the ways we can connect two sentences:

With a semi-colon:

> *Bill is a good student; he studies all the time.*

With a semi-colon and a conjunctive adverb:

> *Bill is a good student; however, he rarely studies.*

With a comma and a coordinating conjunction:

> *Bill is a good student, and he studies all the time.*

You can, of course, add other words to the sentence to connect them:

> *Bill is a good student because he studies all the time.*

> *Bill is a good student who studies all the time.*

What is happening in these last two cases is that the words that have been added actually change the second part of the sentences into incomplete ideas:

> *Because he studies all the time.*

> *Who studies all the time.*

These are not long complete ideas and so they can simply be added to the sentence to become part of the predicate.

C. **The last thing that commas do is to add non-essential, non-sentence information to a sentence**:

> *Clearly, Bill, who is majoring in chemistry, is a good student, when he has time to study.*

In the above, the actual sentence (the complete idea) is

> *Bill is a good student.*

All of the other information—"clearly," "who is majoring in chemistry," and "when he has time to study"—is additional, non-essential information and could be taken off the sentence. This is another job that commas perform: they add non-essential, non-sentence information to a sentence. You can test this by taking off the items that have been attached to the sentence with commas to see if the sentence still works.

The issue of whether or not the information you are adding to a sentence is essential or not can get a bit confusing, of course, and it takes a bit of practice to know whether or not to use the comma to set off that information. Look at the following examples:

My brother, who is in the army, never attended college.

My brother who is in the army never attended college.

In the first example, we are implying that the information "who is in the army" is non-essential because we have surrounded it with commas. This means that the information is merely additional—we may only have one brother and so the information is not essential to identifying which brother we mean. In the second example, we have left off the commas, which implies that the phrase "who is in the army" is essential to identifying which brother we mean. That probably means that we have more than one brother and we need that phrase to help identify what brother we mean.

Making conscious choices about where you will use a comma takes some practice. Remember that commas are used to separate more than two items in a list, to join two sentences together with a coordinating conjunction, or to attach non-essential information to a sentence. Commas generally do not indicate a pause, as many people think.

Sentence—Directness, Clarity, and Sentence Logic

As with all languages, English has a sort of "default" construction for sentences. The standard construction is subject first, then verb, then direct object, complement, or subordinate clause. You will recognize this construction:

Our campus needs more recycling bins.

Bill, his friends, and everyone at the office held a going-away party for Bruce.

Problems with sentence construction often occur because the sentence has been written in some other order or that the actual "actor" and "action" in the sentence are not in the subject and predicate positions:

The proposal of the club was to institute a recycling program for the campus.

This is not a "bad" sentence, but it could be made better. In this example, the word that is the subject of the sentence is "proposal" and the verb is "was." The sentence could be improved by moving the "actor" in the sentence, the club, into the subject position and by moving the action, the act of proposing the recycling program, into the verb position:

The club proposed a recycling program for the campus.

Part of the problem with these kinds of sentences is that verbs have often been turned into nouns: in the original sentence, the verb "to propose" has been turned into the noun "proposal." Watch for these nouns that have been made out of verbs and see if you can use them in their verb forms as the actual verbs of your sentences:

First, the club made the argument for recycling on campus, then they had expectations for the participation of the students.

The key words—the nouns that have been made out of verbs—are "argument," "expectations," and "participation." Look what happens when we transform those nouns back into the verbs of our sentence:

First, the club argued for recycling on campus, then they expected the students to participate.

Sentences can also be made stronger by the use of more "active" verbs:

The campus is now leading recycling efforts in the community, and its students are recycling to help clean up the campus.

In this sentence, the verbs are "is" and "are." We can move key action words into the verb positions of the sentence to make it stronger:

The campus now leads recycling efforts in the community, and its students recycle to help clean up the campus.

Another construction that inhibits sentence clarity is known as **passive voice**. In sentences that use passive voice, the actor in the sentence is transformed into the receiver of the action instead of the actor:

The recycling program is seen by a majority of the students as vital, but the inconvenience of the program has been pointed out by others.

Writers can recognize passive voice constructions by looking for verb constructions that use "is," "are," and other forms of the verb "to be," or constructions that employ "has," "have," and other forms of the verb "to have." Generally, sentences can be improved by moving the actor in the sentence into the subject position. This will generally eliminate the passive voice:

> *The majority of students see the recycling program as vital, but others*
> *point out the program's inconvenience.*

Most sentences, as with most punctuation and word choice problems, can be fixed if the writer will read carefully and consider that almost all sentences can be made more effective with a little bit of consideration and work. Most of the time, the writer does not have to know what the problem is called in order to "fix" it, although having some basic idea about what makes sentences work well will help. The trick is to read your sentences out loud, listen to how they sound, identify the parts of the sentence that do not work, and then fix them. At first, it may take a bit more time to review your own sentences this closely, but that is the essential advantage of writing: the ability to examine what you have written and to make better choices.

CHOOSING VISUAL IMAGES—WHAT DOES IT LOOK LIKE?

The last 30 years have brought about an explosion of technology that has profoundly changed the way we communicate. This technology has made it easy for almost anyone with a few computer skills to access an amazing amount of information, to explore original ideas, and then to create text, photos, videos, and sound to communicate those ideas. Whether you use computers and printers located primarily at school or at home (or both), you most likely have access to technology you can use to design documents containing sophisticated charts, graphs, and images. You can also probably print these documents out in full color or post them to the Internet. Once on the Web, you can create collections of your original work—whether that is text, photos, videos, or whatever—and display that work in portfolios, such as the one you create in this class. You can create blogs, photoblogs, and videoblogs. All these documents and videos and photos can then be linked together through professional and social networking sites. Then, you and others can access all these creations from any location through wireless internet and data downloads to your computer, netbook, or smartphone.

Since most of us grew up in the midst of this explosion, it may seem like a simple thing to click onto the Internet on our desktop, laptop, netbook, or even our smartphone, type a word or phrase into a search engine, and call up hundreds, if not millions, of documents, images, sound, and video on almost any topic. The ability to access such an immense amount of information from such a wide variety of sources allows us to gather different perspectives on any issue or event and to incorporate this information into our own writing in a way that people of the last generation could never have dreamed possible.

Only a few decades ago there were a limited number of informational sources available to the average citizen. Personal knowledge about what was happening in the world was limited by the quality of the local news outlets and by what few national and international television, radio, and print sources were available. Now we can, through cable, satellite, or the Internet, watch and read the news as it is reported in various cities and countries around the world as it happens. Through our televisions, radios, computers, netbooks, smartphones, and hand-held readers we can instantly connect to dozens of local, national, and global news and entertainment sources. Often, the reports we receive are accompanied by images, video, and sound that have been recorded and sent almost immediately from the actual event. Along with these news reports, we can read opinions about what the events of the day mean from various editorialists whose opinions are published almost as the events occur. We can also access blogs from thousands of people who are eager to share their individual experiences with us or to offer their opinions on almost any subject. We can discuss the events of the day with friends, family, and strangers who are hundreds or thousands of miles away almost instantly through email, text-messaging, and on a variety of social networks, blogs, and discussion boards.

All these communication technologies are much more than just simply ways to "keep in touch" with each other. In fact, many consider that Barack Obama's effective use of Facebook, MySpace, Twitter, and instant messaging was instrumental in helping his campaign win the presidential race of 2008. During recent government crackdowns on official media in both Iran and Moldova, microblogging provided the only method of publishing and receiving information to and from dissidents (http://www.thenation.com/blogs/notion/443634) (http://neteffect.foreignpolicy. com/posts/2009/04/07/moldovas_twitter_revolution). Government and non-government agencies and organizations are beginning to understand the importance of social networking and microblogging for setting and promoting domestic and social policy. Advertising firms and corporations now also employ social networking sites, blogs, and microblogs as effective ways to influence public perception about their companies and products.

All this communication can be overwhelming, and even those of us who grew up in the middle of the digital revolution may be left feeling as though we are drowning in a sea of ideas and images. Because of the increased number of perspectives available to us, we have been forced to adapt new ways of reading and writing so that we can more quickly synthesize and understand those various perspectives. Any technological change requires a change in the way people think, and the digital revolution is no exception. A few decades ago, students and professionals needed only to be able to communicate in person or over the phone and to write and read a letter, a report, or an article. Now, students need to add to those skills the ability to communicate through instant messaging, email, microblogging, social networks, and webpages.

Before the printing press was invented, the biggest problem was that each piece of written text had to be created by hand. After Guttenburg invented the printing press (actually what he invented was moveable type), books and pamphlets could be created more quickly and distributed more widely, and so more people learned to read and write. Just as these technological improvements in printing allowed more writers to publish their views, digital media and the Internet now allow anyone with access to "publish" his or her views on any subject on webpages, in blogs, and on social and professional networking sites. In the din of all this information, well-designed documents are a must, as anyone with a moderately powerful computer and the right programs can create imaginative and powerful documents that contain photos, drawings, graphs, color, sound, and video. This makes awareness of how document design and images affect rhetoric—how design and images are "written" and "read"—important to the study of writing.

READING AND WRITING VISUAL IMAGES

It may seem odd that we can talk about "reading" and "writing" images, design, and color, but the fact is that modern theories of rhetoric have been expanded to include these elements. While a comprehensive study of graphic and document design are beyond the scope of this class, we hope that some basic experience with using graphics and images in your work will help you gain greater awareness of the rhetorical power of images and design.

At the most basic level, documents in all genres exhibit design elements that help us understand what kind of text we are reading and what that text means. We expect that newspapers, magazines, and books will look a certain way, and, in spite of the old admonition that you cannot tell a book by its cover, you actually can tell lots about a book by looking at its visual elements. You can at least tell a bit about what kind of a book it is. A romance novel is likely to be designed quite a bit differently than a textbook for your Algebra class.

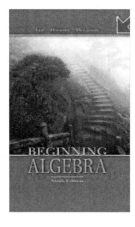

Just as you need to be able to understand how words work to influence readers, you need also to understand how images and the design elements affect the reader. This is because images operate in much the same way as words do. It may be tempting to believe that images contribute to meaning simply by adding more information or by making the information easier to understand, but images and design elements can also contribute to the emotional appeal, the logical appeal, and the credibility of a piece of writing. We may be tempted to trust pictures for the same reason that we tend to trust statistics and "facts": because we believe that pictures, like facts and statistics, cannot "lie." Still, it is appropriate to remember that pictures, just like facts and statistics, can also be chosen or designed specifically to influence the reader's understanding. Just as you must carefully choose the type of text, the type of language, and the type of style you will use to "reach" your reader, so, too, must you consciously and carefully choose the way your documents look and the images that accompany them.

You are most likely familiar with the cliché "a picture is worth a thousand words." As with most clichés, there is a bit of truth involved. Each picture that you choose can—through its images, colors, and composition—convey an amount of information equivalent to many words, and that information can affect the emotional content, the credibility of the author, and the logic of the argument. As an example, examine the following pictures of the 44th President of the United State, Barack Obama, and notice how each of the images has been "written" to promote a specific "reading" about the President and the values he represents.

Barack Obama

Barack Obama and Superman

Barack Obama
playing basketball

Obama One at http://commons.wikimedia.org/wiki/File:Jurvetson__Barack_Obama_on_the_Primary_(by).jpg
Obama Two at http://commons.wikimedia.org/wiki/File:Barack_Obama_with_Superman.jpg.
Obama Three at http://commons.wikimedia.org/wiki/File:BarackObama-Basketball.JPEG

In each of the pictures to the left, a different story is portrayed about "who" Barack Obama is and what values he might represent. As you examine the photos, pay attention to how elements of color and composition affect the message. Even the backgrounds in each of these pictures contributes to a particular "reading" of the image.

Now examine three photographs depicting the popular singer, Michael Jackson, whose recent death was a significant news item in 2009.

Michael Jackson?   Michael Jackson and the Reagans

Michael Jackson

Were you fooled at all by photo number one? Does it matter that the person who "is" Michael Jackson in the first photo is not the actual person?

CULTURAL AWARENESS IN MEDIA REPRESENTATIONS

Recently, government agencies, publishers, and many businesses have begun to demand that writers who are employed to create brochures, textbooks, and webpages include people from diverse ethnic and social backgrounds. Generally, writers and image-makers are also required to include representations of both genders in pictures that accompany official documents. While there is no need to balance every image as far as gender and ethnicity is concerned, some awareness of these cultural issues is wise even if it is not required. Some may object that this is simply "political correctness," but the truth is that more women and people from varied backgrounds are now employed in government positions and in the workplace. As such, images that accompany official government and business documents now generally promote inclusion of people of diverse ethnicities and represent an awareness of gender equity. Whatever you think of this development, it is important to maintain an awareness of the rhetorical significance of whatever images you choose to add to your writing.

A ▶ Activity

Examine the following images and analyze how they represent the concept of adult illiteracy and how each might be used in an essay about adult illiteracy.

Adult Illiteracy in America

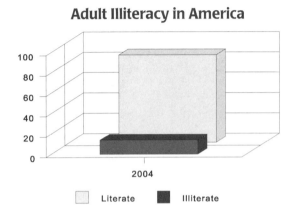

Literate   Illiterate

Adult Illiteracy in America

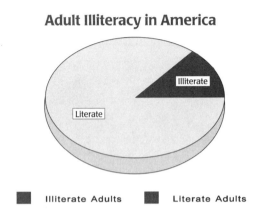

Illiterate Adults   Literate Adults

Adult Illiteracy in America

Illiterate Adults   Literate Adults

Adult Illiteracy in America

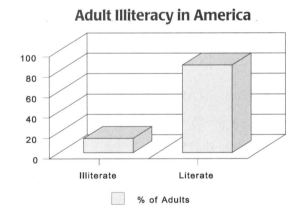

% of Adults

Adult Literacy is Important

Literate Adults Can Read Books

Literate People Can Fill Out Important
Forms

✓CHECKLIST OF QUESTIONS FOR VISUALS

1. What kind of visual element have you added to your project? A graph or chart, a video, or a picture or illustration?

2. How does the visual you've chosen add to the *ethos, pathos,* or *logos* of your argument?

3. Does the visual primarily add support to your argument as an example or does it illustrate the primary theme?

4. Does your visual represent the "whole story," or has it been slanted to present one side?

5. Does your visual take into account multi-cultural and cross-cultural issues?

GLOSSARY OF TERMS

analytical structures - structures that present and evaluate information

argumentative structures - structures that synthesize narrative and analysis into sound and believable explanations, arguments, or proposals

backing - the details that make the warrants work.

blogging - to test out their writing on real readers in a more informal context

branding - refers to using the specific names of things—the "brands"—to strengthen the description

claim -the purpose of your argument; what you want the reader to think, consider, feel, or do as a result of reading your argument.

conventions - the way things are normally done

demographic - a statistic characterizing human populations (or segments of human populations broken down by age or sex or income etc.)

dialogue - a strategy to strengthen your narrative by using a person's own words

discourse communities - the various language groups that people encounter on a daily basis

drafting - the second step in the writing process; writing a first version to be filled out and polished later

ethos - the writer's credibility

exigency - the situation that motivates a writer to write

freewriting - sitting in front of the computer or with pen and

genre - the different categories of texts that are available to writers. For instance, letters, emails, reports, websites, essays, articles, and books are all genres—or categories—of non-fiction writing. Novels, short stories, poems, and plays are all genres of fiction writing.

grounds - the basic statistics, facts, or evidence that the reader needs to accept in order to respond positively to your claim.

idea-clustering - similar to list-making except the major idea for the writing project is generally put in the center of the paper and the supporting ideas are arranged around the major idea with spokes to connect them. Further supports for those ideas are then arranged around them.

ideal community of readers - consists of people who are already interested in the topic or who might be persuaded to become interested in the topic

journaling - can be an especially effective way to prewrite because it gives the writer a way to test out ideas, sentences, and strategies before committing to a large project

list-making - plan for a writing project by making a list of your major ideas and then list below or next to those major ideas what your supporting ideas and points might be

literacy narrative - how people have learned to read and write

logos - the logic of the argument or persuasion

media critique - writing about the media; however, is not meant to imply that only negative things must be said

narrative structures - using structures that present stories and experiences

outlining - a kind of list in which items are indented to show how they are grouped under or equivalent to other ideas. You can use a standard numbering and lettering system for an outline.

paraphrasing - putting the author's major idea into your own words

pathos - the reader's emotions

planning - plan what you are going to write before you write it

prewriting - the first step in the writing process; the creation and arrangement of ideas preliminary to writing

proofing (sometimes referred to as editing) - (also proofreading) traditionally means reading a copy of a text in order to detect and correct any errors

qualifiers and rebuttals - the modifications and restrictions you put upon your claim and warrants

recursive - steps that often overlap and fold back upon each other

revising - read what you have written to see if you can make it more effective

rhetor - a master or teacher of rhetoric; an orator

rhetoric - using language effectively to please or persuade; the strategic use of language

thesis - the purpose of the writing

usage conventions - describes the way words are most frequently used in the English language and the way sentences are generally put together by actual writers

warrants - the reasons why the grounds justifies the claim; the major supporting points of your argument.

writing process - a set of steps that a writer takes in order to create a writing project

WEBSITE INDEX

Choices 2.0 Online Portal
http://www.choicesportal.com

Introduction

Malcolm Gladwell's book, *Outliers*
http://www.gladwell.com/outliers/index.html

Wikimedia Commons
http://en.wikipedia.org/wiki/Wikimedia_Commons

Chapter 1

The Scientific Method
http://biology.clc.uc.edu/courses/bio104/SCI_meth.htm

Blogger
http://www.blogger.com

Wordpress
http://www.wordpress.org

Youtube
http://www.youtube.com

Social networking sites
http://www.facebook.com
http://www.myspace.com
http://www.twitter.com

Flickr
http://www.flickr.com

Fotolog
http://www.fotolog.com

Rhetorical Questions from Brigham Young University
http://rhetoric.byu.edu/figures/R/rhetorical%20questions.htm

A First Look at the Literacy of America's Adults in the 21st Century
http://nces.ed.gov/NAAL/PDF/2006470_1.PDF

Chapter 2

Online Gaming Community Sites
http://www.doomworld.com
http://halo.bungie.org

Fansites
http://steveearle.net
http://www.lilkimzone.com

Great Seal of the United States
http://www.greatseal.com

National Center for Education Statistics
http://nces.ed.gov

Wikimedia Commons
http://commons.wikimedia.org/wiki/Main_Page

Sample Blog Search Engines
Blogdigger
http://www.blogdigger.com
Feedster
http://www.feedster.com
Technorati
http://www.technorati.com)

Chapter 3

James Frey
http://www.thesmokinggun.com/archive/0104061jamesfrey1.html

Purdue's On-line Writing Lab
http://owl.english.purdue.edu/owl/resource/588/01/

Literacy Matters - Cause and Effect
http://www.literacymatters.org/content/text/cause.htm

Toulmin Model of Argument, sponsored by Colorado State University
http://changingminds.org/disciplines/argument/making_argument/toulmin.htm

Chapter 5

Oracle of Bacon, University of Virgina
http://oracleofbacon.org/

Chapter 6

Marlboro Man
http://adage.com/century/icon01.html

How the Brain responds to color
http://www.colormatters.com/brain.html

Chapter 7

Bureau of Labor Statistics
http://www.bls.gov

Supplements

Non-Faked Moon Landing
http://pirlwww.lpl.arizona.edu/~jscotti /NOT_faked

Family Values, Killer Industries: Whose Family, What Values?
http://www.citizen.org/congress/campaign/archive/articles.cfm?ID=5421>

Microblogging in Iraq and Moldova
http://www.thenation.com/blogs/notion/443634

http://neteffect.foreignpolicy.com/posts/2009/04/07/moldovas_twitter_
revolution

At the time of printing, all of these sites were active.

INDEX